To Dorothy Ellen Rose Malloy Cook
(just so there'd be no doubt)

Acknowledgments

Several thousand people belong in this section. I'll never get them all in.

Bill Brohaugh saw the title and knew there was a book behind it.

Catherine Brohaugh helped keep the book true to the title.

So many master writers have helped me grow. Ben Logan and Harper Lee showed the power of the child remembering. Herb Gardner created Murray Burns, who knew to name each day and make it his own. James Goldman asserted that holding to your vision might make you lonely, but it doesn't make you wrong.

My list of writer-heroes includes Ken Kesey, Natalie Goldberg, Larry McMurtry, Mark Twain, William Saroyan and Sam and Porter Harvey. You may not have heard of those last two. They write clear, honest copy and the best obituaries in the world for the Guntersville, Alabama *Advertiser-Gleam*.

These people nourish me:

• Chuck Jones, Bob Clampett and Jay Ward made all those wonderful cartoons, and Mel Blanc made so many of them talk.

• Katharine Hepburn, Spencer Tracy and John Wayne played all those parts while refusing to be anybody but themselves.

• Soupy Sales took a pie in the face for us all.

• Bret Maverick and Sergeant Bilko tested the limits.

• "Pistol" Pete Maravich and "Hot Rod" Huntley played basketball with uncommon originality.

• The Lone Ranger, Hoppy, Superman, Davy Crockett and Captain Marvel were brave always and did what was right.

• "Big D" and Sandy, "Hondo" and Willie D., "Duke" and "Junior" and Carlos and all the rest played baseball, which is all they needed to do.

• Mason Williams wrote "Cowboy Buckaroo," as fine a statement of a philosophy of life as I have ever encountered.

Friends have taught me much.

Bruce Allison taught me how to look at trees, and Shiela Reaves taught me to sling a pretend camera over my shoulder and look at everything more intently.

HOW TO WRITE
WITH THE
SKILL
OF A MASTER
AND THE
GENIUS
OF A CHILD

MARSHALL J. COOK

Writer's
Digest
Books

Cincinnati, Ohio

About the Author

Marshall is a writer and teacher, which is what he always wanted to be. He has published articles in national magazines from *U.S. Catholic* to *Law and Order*. He is a regular contributor to *Madison Magazine*.

As a professor for the University of Wisconsin-Madison Outreach, he teaches 60 seminars a year on writing and creativity. He's also a frequent speaker at writing conferences.

He has self-published *Writing for the Joy of It* under the label Will Beymer Press, and his first book for Writer's Digest Books is titled *Freeing Your Creativity: A Writer's Guide*. He's currently at work on a new book, *Slow Down and Get More Done*.

Marshall reads, watches television, jogs, lifts weights and rides an exercise bike that refuses to move. He is a passionate baseball fan.

He and wife Ellen have a son, Jeremiah, and live in Madison, Wisconsin with their schnauzer, Rosie, and two Persian kittens, Ralph and Norton.

How to Write With the Skill of a Master and the Genius of a Child. Copyright © 1992 by Marshall J. Cook. Printed and bound in the United States of America. All rights reserved. No part of this book may be reproduced in any form or by any electronic or mechanical means including information storage and retrieval systems without permission in writing from the publisher, except by a reviewer, who may quote brief passages in a review. Published by Writer's Digest Books, an imprint of F&W Publications, Inc., 1507 Dana Avenue, Cincinnati, Ohio 45207. 1-800-289-0963. First edition.

96 95 94 93 92   5 4 3 2 1

Library of Congress Cataloging in Publication Data

Cook, Marshall J.
    How to write with the skill of a master and the genius of a child/Marshall J. Cook. — 1st ed.
        p.   cm.
    Includes index.
    ISBN 0-89879-529-X
    1. Authorship   I. Title.
    PN151.C645   1992
    808'.02 — dc20   92-7884
                                                                CIP

Designed by Clare Finney
Cover illustration by Betsy Japour

Blake Kellogg continues to discuss life and Life with me and has shared more miles in a state fleet car than either of us dares to calculate.

My students, and especially Dave Fox and Betsy Anderson, let me share part of their writing journeys.

Thanks to Bill Rivers, Stanley Sheinkopf and my other master teachers.

Special thanks to my parents, my first and best mentors, and to my son, Jeremiah, who shared his childhood with me and who remembers those long walks by the river.

All the writing and thinking and reading and teaching and goofing and playing revolves around my wife, Ellen. We are partners and companions on the journey. Whatever comes next, we'll meet it together.

Contents

Introduction: Learning to Be Ignorant

No one who bothers about originality will ever be original, whereas if you try simply to tell the truth, you will, nine times out of ten, become original without ever having noticed it.
— C.S. Lewis

You may or may not have been a beautiful baby, but I'll bet you were a passionate one. You no doubt arrived with plenty of personality and loads of strong preferences as to how the world should be run. You may not have known much about this new world you'd been thrust into, but you were willing and eager to learn.

We call such a state "ignorance." We equate it with bliss, and we mistake it for stupidity, although it is neither.

You didn't stay ignorant long. You learned so rapidly that to miss a minute of your development was to miss several milestones: the day you found your toes; the day you first smiled (or passed gas, or whatever baby giggles really signify); the day you rolled over, with just a little help; the day you said "Mama" (or "Schrumpf," which was close enough).

You accomplished your astonishing early learning without teachers or texts, simply by applying your incredible powers of concentration to the world within and without you. There was nothing quite as intense as your stare. "Oh," you seemed to be saying. "So this is what the world is all about."

Soon your universe expanded beyond the crib, and you became absorbed in the ground-level wonders of sticks and stones and candy wrappers, the treasures an adult walks right past without seeing.

I revisited this child's world while taking my toddler son, Jeremiah, for his early morning walk — up the hill to the local playground to try out the swings, down the hill, past a field full of cows, to the train trestle and the Napa River and our ultimate destination, Partrick's Candy Store. Alone, the walk would have taken me fifteen minutes (except that, alone, I never would have taken the walk at all). With Jeremiah, it was the work of a morning. A type-A, goal-oriented adult had to learn to adapt his stride to the starts and stops of a curious child. For me, it was a walk. For Jeremiah, it was an adventure. I'll bet you were that way as a kid, too.

Soon, of course, your means of gathering information about the world expanded to include asking questions — *lots* of questions.

"Whatcha doing?"

"How come?"

"What's that for?"

"Can I try it?"

You needed to put a name to everything. And you needed to know why.

You learned to walk and talk, to tie your shoes, and open the cookie jar without making any noise. You learned that Mom's "Ask your father" meant "No," and that Dad's "No" sometimes meant "Maybe."

As you continued on your journey, you mastered many skills — to drive a car or a golf ball, to run a household or a small business, to read textbooks and body English and the ways of a brook trout rising to strike a fly. But none of these lessons match in complexity your earliest lessons, as you acquired the foundation skills and understandings you now take for granted.

As a child, you learned without conscious effort or even awareness. But as you got older, your efforts became more self-conscious and more structured. The learning often became secondary, a means to an end — good grades, a diploma or degree, a job or job advancement. The judgment of others became more important than your own. You learned to learn, not for the inherent joy of it, but to please others. Learning — and failing to learn — began to involve anxiety and pain.

I have a recurring nightmare that I am late for a test in junior high school. The halls are empty. Everyone else is in class, where I'm supposed to be, and I can't remember my locker combination! Do you still get that one, too? It's been a long time since I've darkened the halls of a junior high school. That's some long-lasting anxiety.

Perhaps you learned how to parse a sentence and to analyze the symbolism in Mark Twain's *Huckleberry Finn*. Or perhaps you learned, instead, that you "aren't very good in English" and inwardly decided never to seek the nourishment of a good novel again.

But still you learned and grew, sometimes with the help of teachers, sometimes despite their interference.

Starting the Journey to Becoming a Master

If you were lucky, and if you got the guidance you needed when you needed it, and in a form you could recognize and accept, you may have found your true vocation, the work and play you were meant to do. If so, by applying great energy and concentration to the chore you were given to do, and bringing your inclinations and talents to the task, you started on the road to becoming a master.

The master creates with precision and passion. She has learned the rules and the structures and has learned, too, when to cast rules and structures aside. She performs with uncommon skill and insight and often, too, with uncommon intensity and involvement.

I hope you're striving to become a master writer. Why aim for anything less? You wouldn't want to stop halfway up the mountain, when the view from the top will be so much more beautiful and complete.

The master you seek to become would seem to be the opposite of the child you once were. The child knew nothing, at least in the beginning. The developing master knows much, about her craft and about her world. The child was unreflective and lived wholly in the moment. The master has much experience to draw on in the act of creation. The child was unruly and inefficient. The master is intensely focused and fiercely disciplined.

And yet, at the moment when the master creates, she is like a child. She empties herself of all knowing, lets go of "experience" and preconceived "truth" and lets her inner vision guide her — just as a child trusts intuition and plays with unself-conscious originality. Knowing so much about life and about the craft of writing, the master forgets what she knows and becomes ignorant and guileless.

How to Use This Book to Rediscover Your Child
You can draw on the child within you to help you become the master who is also within you. Using your child's intensity and joyful aban-

don, you can create with orginality and brilliance.

To help you explore your inner gifts, I'll share my experiences and the experiences of other writers and masters I've been honored to know. But your truth won't come from me or from any other so-called expert. You must experience your own truth and learn to trust and follow that truth.

Please don't absorb my words passively. Engage them. Test and adapt the lessons you find here. Hold them up against your own intuitions and experience. When my words contradict what you feel to be true about yourself, trust your intuitions.

I'll be inviting you to participate in a series of explorations. They involve writing, often of a fanciful and free nature, and then reflecting on what the writing reveals about yourself. I urge you not to skip these opportunities. Your learning and your growth are in them. They'll allow you to find your path.

Get a special notebook just for these explorations. Set aside certain times and places for them. Make them an event.

I'll be doing all of them with you. Some of my explorations will be "kitchen table papers," written in my yellow spiral journal at the kitchen table second thing in the morning (after the jog or the pedaling on the bike that goes nowhere in the basement), with the coffee brewing and the dog bringing me her plastic toys to throw.

I'll write others after walking or biking to work. On a warm day, I'll get my coffee in the student union at the University of Wisconsin-Madison, where I teach, and sit on the terrace overlooking Lake Mendota and write as freely and honestly as I can. On the cold mornings (the other ten months of the year), I'll hole up in a little coffeehouse called Steep & Brew on State Street, where the coffee is stronger and more flavorful but the view considerably less expansive.

These writings will sustain and energize me, as journal-keeping always has. They'll help to carry me into the day, with all of its demands. They'll teach and remind me what the rest of the day is for.

Your explorations will do that for you, too.

So don't charge through each chapter and hurry on to the next. It isn't that kind of book. Linger with the ideas. Don't just read this book. Do it.

■ ■ ■ ■ ■ ■ ■ ■ ■ ■ ■ ■ ■ ■ ■ ■ ■ ■
Exploration: Becoming the Child Remembering

 Narrate a childhood experience. Try not to write *about* the experience. Re-create it, just as you remember it. You don't have to comment on the experience or draw any particular lesson from it. The experience contains its own significance and needs no further justification.

Don't worry about being "accurate." All memory is creative, subjective and selective. Let yourself create.

Layer your narrative with specific detail. Work in the smells and textures.

If you have trouble getting started, make a list of experiences you might write about and choose the one that seems the most interesting. You can stop and rechoose if you like, and you can certainly write about more than one experience if you find this exploration to be useful or fun or both.

As you write, you'll probably become at least two different people—the child you remember yourself to have been and the adult remembering that child. Ben Logan's *The Land Remembers* and Harper Lee's *To Kill a Mockingbird* are marvelous examples of this kind of writing.

As you relax into the writing, a third person may emerge— the child remembering. This is a wonderful being. Let it take over if it will.

This exploration will help you to touch the child within you and to let that child begin to nurture, teach and liberate you as a master writer.

Don't Read on Until You've Finished Your Exploration

You've probably read many textbooks with exercises in them followed by answers to those exercises. This isn't that kind of book. I'll include many examples of explorations. Some will be my own, and some will come from writer-friends of mine. I include them simply to let you see how others are doing on their journeys and to show you other possibilities.

Don't compare your writing to the writing you find here or to anybody else's writing. Such comparisons are useless at best. And they can be disheartening and damaging. If I compare my rough drafts and beginning explorations to the polished work of a master, my work will seem crude and awkward. I might conclude that I'm not "good enough" and stop doing the work I was meant to do. What a mistake that would be.

You'll find no models of perfection here, no "right answers." There are only your answers. Only you can teach yourself how to write openly and honestly, from the child who has always been and the master who is emerging within you.

So please read these segments for what they are, explorations from your fellow writers, who are teaching themselves the lessons they must learn just as you are teaching yourself everything you must know to be the writer you must become.

Here's one of my explorations into a childhood experience.

The Child Remembers Catching the Monster Fish

He woke me in the still dark.

"On deck all the fishermen," he whispered, so as not to awaken my mother, sleeping in the next room.

I hadn't slept well. Later I learned that he hadn't either. He was wakeful from anticipation, I'm sure, I from dread. What was I scared of? That I would disappoint him? I think yes. And perhaps I was scared, too, of being bored, trapped out on that little rowboat for hours. I feared boredom in those days, having not yet gained the adult habit of carrying a book with me always.

He had all the gear ready, of course. He spent most of his not-fishing hours while on vacation getting ready to fish.

I fumbled into my clothes and stumbled behind him down the steep slope to the dock and to our rented rowboat. I'm sure I heard the scolding of the blue jays and the dialogue of the birds I knew only to call "Whosits," after a song my mother had taught me. And I must have absorbed the good pine smell and the sensation, not quite smell, of the clean mountain air.

Dad rowed strong and steady, the way he did everything. Never did it occur to me, in all of my growing up, that my father was getting older, or that his muscles might ache sometimes, the way mine do now. He could row forever and never get tired and never lose his way in the darkness.

I huddled in the bow in my jacket and life preserver, probably feeling sorry for myself. I spent a great deal of my childhood feeling put upon. It couldn't have been cold, even at this high altitude, in the midst of a Southern California summer, but I'm pretty sure I shivered.

The dock slipped away. The dark outline of the shore glided smoothly past on my right. I heard only the liquid dip of oars in water.

He knew where to anchor. He had patiently scouted the Lake, had talked to the old-timers in the bait and tackle shop in the Village, had watched others to see who caught fish and who just sat. He remembered exactly where he was and how far off the bottom his hooks had been when he caught fish.

He rigged my line and baited my hook first. He may have used Velveeta cheese or Plautzke's fireballs or maybe even the "secret formula" he concocted at home.

Was I old enough to cast for myself? I think he let me try. He showed me again how to release the drag on the reel and to hold a loop of line with my forefinger, how to draw the rod back and snap it forward, propelling the bait, sinker, leader and line out in a soft arc, the bait and leader hitting the smooth water with a soft "plop."

Except that the bait was no longer attached to the hook. I had forgotten to let go of the line as I cast and jerked the bait off.

"Right in the hole," he might have said when, on the third or fourth or tenth try, I managed to get bait and line into the water together.

How much of what follows do I actually remember, and how much is really my father's telling and retelling of the story? I can't be sure. I remember how still the lake was in the pale light of false dawn. I remember the silhouette of the pines along the shore. I remember the gentle movement of the boat responding to the shiftings of our bodies. And I remember the mystic, cosmic tug on my line.

Had I really felt something?

The universe held its breath and waited with me.

I felt it again, a quick tug, then nothing. I watched the tip of my rod as if to glance away meant sudden, painful death.

I found my voice.

"Dad! I think I got a bite!"

He was rigging his line. Rigging the lines took precedence over all other tasks. "Can't catch a fish without a line in the water," he told me often. I have since come to understand that this philosophy, along with many of his other teachings, had applications far beyond fishing.

I'll bet he had to fight the urge to take my pole from me. I know I had to fight the urge to thrust it at him.

He had coached me about waiting for the right moment and then setting the hook. His own hook-setting was so sudden and so violent, it often scared me, and I was sure he would yank the fish right out of the water and over our heads.

When was the right moment? He couldn't teach me that. I had to feel it. I'd yanked too soon or too late and come up with a limp line so often. So much in life is timing. So much is touch. So much of what we must learn can't be taught.

Now! Something inside me screamed in response to the triple-quick bump in my fingertips. Now! I desperately jerked up on the pole, clinging to it for my life, all the while dreading the dejection that was sure to follow. But there was instead a furious tugging. Line was whirring steadily from my reel. The fish was on—and fighting.

"Keep the tip up."

If you allow slack in the line, the fish can spit the hook. He may not, must not spit the hook.

I don't know how long the fish and I fought, the fish for its life, I for something that seemed at least as important. It seemed an hour but was surely much less as I slowly gained back line, letting the splendid life play itself out on the other end. I didn't want to kill it. But Lord, how I wanted, needed to catch it.

The fish broke water, near the boat. The newly risen sun glittered its scales. I dared to hope, then, for my father had told me that once they surfaced, their gills would fill with air, and the fight would go out of them.

My father leaned out as far as he could, keeping the lip of the net just below the water's surface. By magic—surely someone else's hands were guiding the fish now—the fish glided steadily, inevitably, head just out of the water, into the net.

My father worked quickly, skillfully. First he thrust his thumb into the fish's mouth and deftly broke its neck. He wanted no suffering. He thrust the red dehooker down the gullet and retrieved my hook. He held the fish in the cold lake water. And then he held the fish high, forefinger hooked through the gill, showing him to me — and to the other fishermen in nearby boats whose arrival I hadn't even noticed.

When my father was especially happy with me, he said, "Atta boy, Shorty." I suppose he said that now. "Shorty" was his nickname for me even long after I grew to meet him eye-to-eye. It derived from my place at the end of the family anchor chain — the "short shot" in naval parlance — and not to my stature.

Before he put my fish in the creel with the wet rags to keep it fresh, he got the tape measure out of the tackle box. Thirteen and a half inches. A monster. I think it's still the largest trout I've ever caught. Later he would record the record breaker in his fishing log, where he noted all our fish and our camping trips and other milestones of our lives together. I have his log now, and I wouldn't trade it for all the world's wealth.

He told and retold the story of how I caught the great rainbow trout at dawn, before he even got his line in the water. I heard the pride in his voice each time he told it.

I can hear it still.

1

Learning to Say
"I Am Not You"

To be original, you must listen to the voice of your own heart rather than the clamor of the world—and have the courage to teach publicly what you have learned. The source of all genius is sincerity.
—Ludwig Borne

You probably went through the "No!" Mania, perhaps as a part of that tumultuous stage known as "the terrible twos." "No!" (always with the exclamation point) might even have been the first word you discovered. (I have a sister-in-law whose first word was "Adlai," but that's another story.) But even if you began with "Mama" or "Dada," I'll bet you soon embraced "No!" as your all-purpose response to every question.

If you're going through the "No!" Mania with a child of your own (nature's revenge?), don't worry. Those who supposedly understand these things tell us that all that "No"-ing simply means "I am not you." It's a necessary step, part of the declaration of independence each child must make.

But the world soon begins to challenge our fledgling sense of independence. We go to school and learn the Right Way to do things.

Learning to Say No Again

Time for a pop quiz. Books on the floor. Pencils at the ready. Eyes on your own paper. Go.

1. "I" before "E" except after _____.
2. Never end a sentence with a _____.
3. Never split a(n) _____.

If you answered 1. "C," 2. "preposition," and 3. "infinitive," you've remembered your lessons well. You get a gold star, and you may stay after class to clean the erasers.

Now answer one more question.

4. Sez who? _____.

Daring to Boldly Defy the Rulemakers

Who decided, for example, that "I" comes before "E" except after "C" ("or when sounded like 'A' as in 'neighbor' and 'weigh' ")? In Shakespeare's day, you could pretty much spell things however you pleased, so long as a reader could figure out what you meant. "Nabor"? No problem. Probably makes more sense than the "right" way, which doesn't make a lot of sense at all and is thus hard to learn.

But along came the dictionary makers, who decided that, for the sake of consistency (and, I suppose, to sell dictionaries), we'd better have a right way (or maybe two, as with the acceptance of the British variant of "colour" for "color"). If the occasional maverick like "height" seems to defy all the rules, well, won't that sell more dictionaries?

The rule against ending a sentence with a preposition began with a seventeenth-century poet named John Dryden, who studied Latin and decided that, since "preposition" means "that which goes before," you couldn't very well have a preposition that didn't go before anything. Fine for Dryden, fine for Latin, and fine for the seventeenth century, but not so fine for you and me trying to write with clarity and passion in the here and now. It's really a silly rule, when you think about it, and strict adherence to it can have comically awful results, as with the famous retort to Dryden's rule, attributed in various sources to Winston Churchill, George Bernard Shaw, Oscar Wilde and others: "That's the kind of nonsense up with which I will not put."

Nobody seems to know for sure who first created the rule about splitting infinitives and chiseled it onto a stone tablet. Whoever it was, he or she obviously wasn't a "Star Trek" fan and had never dared "to boldly go where no man has gone before." That sentence splits an infinitive *and* ends with a preposition, and we still manage, somehow, to understand it.

Sometimes you've got to make up your own rules.

"I" before "E" except after eating red onions.

Never end a sentence with a proposition.

Never split an inseam.

Are these rules wrong? Sez who? Only one person has your answers. You do. I'm not advocating anarchy here. Sure, we've got to spell the words right. And we dangle our modifiers and splice our commas at the risk of breaking trust with our readers. But I am advocating that we learn to ask the right question about our language: not "Is it right?" but "Does it work?"

Writing Something Nobody Else Ever Wrote

Kids don't worry about being original. They say things their way, based on their world as they see it, and so, of course, they're original, every one of them. They don't worry about their "style" or "voice." The words just pop out.

Then they hit adolescence, and they all start to talk the same talk. Often they take their verbal cues from cultural icons like Madonna or Bart Simpson. "Teenage-ese" can be as vital and vibrant a jargon as our society produces, but the individuals who speak it don't show much originality in its usage.

By the time we emerge as adults, we have to work at being original. We've learned the clichés and the jargon, and it's temptingly easy to use them when we write. We know we should express our unique perceptions and feelings in a unique way, to do them justice and to offer the reader something worthy of her time. But it's a lot more work.

So much of the good stuff has already been taken. All by himself, Shakespeare used up "Neither a borrower nor a lender be," "To thine own self be true" and dozens of other quotable quotes. You can write "Youth is wasted on the young" (not Shakespeare, this time, but Shaw), but you can't pretend to have made it up yourself.

What do you imagine the odds are that you could sit down right now and compose a sentence that has never been written just that way in the entire history of writing? Is such a thing even possible?

Actually, it's a sure thing.

Why You Can't Help but Be Original

Peter Farb makes a startling point in his book *Word Play*. According to Farb, the sentence I just wrote about him has undoubtedly never been written before in the entire history of the English language.

And neither has the sentence I just wrote about the first sentence I just wrote.

We can prove Farb's point with a little simple math (the only kind I'm willing to engage in). Suppose we only had two nouns and two verbs in the English language. Two nouns: *Johnny* and *chicken*. Two verbs: *cluck* and *sneeze*. According to my calculations, if we don't factor in any verb tenses, this vocabulary yields just four possible sentences:

1. Chicken clucks.
2. Johnny sneezes.
3. Chicken sneezes.
4. Johnny clucks.

Kind of limits the possibilities for creating great literature, doesn't it? (I think I had a first-grade reader based on this vocabularly.)

Now suppose there are not just two, but 1,000 nouns to choose from. There are many times that number, but to keep things simple, let's limit the discussion to 1,000. And let's give ourselves 1,000 verbs to hook up with those 1,000 nouns. Mathematically, 1,000 nouns times 1,000 verbs produces one million possible two-word sentence combinations. Now Johnny can not only cluck and sneeze. He can rage and roar, belch and hiccup. And so can Horace, Hilda and Constance.

We can use those 1,000 nouns all over again as objects (*Johnny strangled the chicken*) or predicate nominatives (*Johnny is a chicken*). Now we can make 1,000 times 1,000 times 1,000, or one billion sentences.

Throw in 1,000 adjectives to spice up the stew. Now those chickens can be scrawny or plump, obstreperous or quiescent. And now you have a trillion possible combinations.

Throwing out the formula sentences we use so often to carry water for us ("Wish you were here," "Hot enough for you?"), if I compose a sentence made up of a subject noun, a verb, a direct object noun, and an adjective for that noun (I'll throw in the article for nothing), odds are a trillion to one, even in our limited language universe, that I've created something new. No number of monkeys (or fellow writers) pushing the keys on any number of typewriters (or word processors) for an infinite number of years will ever duplicate that sentence.

That's not to say that the sentence will be insightful or meaningful or stirring. That's another matter all together, the matter we should really be concerning ourselves with.

Let's stop worrying about originality and style and just concern ourselves with saying something worth saying.

Coloring Outside the Lines

You learned more than grammar in grammar school. You also learned rules of right behavior that would enable you to get along with the other kids and to get by with the teachers. Getting by meant sitting still, keeping quiet, and turning your assignments in on time. It meant getting "four" every time you added two and two. It meant coloring inside the lines and making sure your sky was blue and your grass green—even if you might have thought green sky and blue grass would be nice for a change. You learned to stand in line, to take turns, and to share your toys. You could disobey, of course, but if you did, you paid a price.

As you grew up, life kept teaching you these sorts of lessons. You learned, for example, that it's wise to share your boss's political beliefs—or at least to appear to do so. You're still free to disagree, and you still pay a price, only now the price tag has become much higher.

Poet e.e. cummings says that the hardest job in the world is to be yourself, while the world tries so hard to make you into somebody else.

Being yourself seems to come easy for kids. They never even have to think about it. They just are. But the adult who is authentically, passionately free of others' definitions is rare enough to be worth celebrating—and making a movie about.

Tilting at Windmills

A character played by George C. Scott in the movie *They Might Be Giants* believes himself to be Sherlock Holmes. Doctors believe him to be incurably psychotic. His brother wants him committed—the better to claim control of the family fortune. Meanwhile "Holmes" pursues clues to the whereabouts of his archenemy, the evil Professor Moriarty.

Dr. Mildred Watson, played by Joanne Woodward, at first attempts to cure him but winds up falling in love with him. Early in their relationship, she asks, "Do many people call you Holmes?"

"No," Holmes says with a frown. "Scarcely anyone."

"That must make you very much alone," Watson says.

"It does that," Holmes admits. "But it doesn't make me wrong."

Don Quixote's windmills, James Goldman tells us in his screenplay, just may be giants after all. And no matter what we think we see, we must remain true to our visions.

Naming the Days

Murray Burns is, to say the least, an original.

"You want to be your own boss," his nephew and ward, Nick, tells him, "but you don't pay yourself anything."

As played pixie-perfect by Jason Robards, Jr. in the movie *A Thousand Clowns*, Murray tries to wring "all the wild possibilities" from life. "If most things aren't funny," he tells his brother, Arnold, "then . . . it's one long dental appointment."

He answers the phone with "Is this good news or money?" and hangs up if it isn't. He celebrates the birthday of Irving R. Feldman, proprietor of a local kosher deli, as his own personal national holiday. He sees cruise ships off, even though he doesn't know anybody on board. "I don't get jealous that way," he explains to Dr. Sandra Markowitz, a psychiatric social worker assigned to check up on Murray's suitability as a guardian. She winds up falling in love with Murray (there seems to be a pattern in these movies) and stays to share the life her colleague dubs "libertine self-indulgence."

"Isn't it great," he tells her, "to find out how many Sandras there are?" Out they come, he says, like a thousand clowns pouring out of the little car at the circus, "whooping and hollering and raising hell."

When Sandy suggests that Murray return to reality, he insists he'll "only go as a tourist." But tourist or no, Murray does return, retaking his old job as head writer for Leo Herman, alias Chuckles the Chipmunk, so he can keep custody of Nick (also known as King, Rover, Big Sam, Chevrolet and The Phantom, among other names. Murray is allowing him to choose his own first name). Murray wants to make sure, he says, that the boy will never "chicken out on himself" and "become one of the dead people." Nick must always know "why he was born a human being and not a chair."

"I gotta know what day it is," he tells his brother, Arnold. "You gotta own your own days, and name them, or else the years go by, and none of them belong to you."

Playwright Herb Gardner doesn't give Murray all the good lines.

"I'm lucky. I'm gifted. I have a talent for surrender," Arnold responds. "But you? You're cursed." Drawing himself up for a rare last word with his brother, Arnold announces, "I'm the best possible Arnold Burns."

Eccentric writer Murray and conservative businessman Arnold both must be their best possible selves. And Nick—or Murray, as he finally has printed on his library card—must name himself along with the days.

Irrational? Probably. Crazy? Maybe. But characters like Murray Burns are surely original, and in their originality and their fierce determination to be themselves, despite the world's best efforts to make them into somebody else, we can see the basis of our own creativity.

"The creative individual," according to researcher Frank Barron, "not only respects the irrational in himself, but courts the most promising source of novelty in his own thought. . . . The creative person is both more primitive and more cultured, more destructive and more constructive, crazier and saner, than the average person."

We are each a mixture of naive, intuitive child and experienced, reasonable adult. Being more creative isn't a matter of letting one dominate the other or even of bringing the two seemingly contradictory facets of our natures into balance. To be more creative, we must be more—more spontaneous child, more considered adult—more authentically ourselves, *all* of ourselves.

Setting the Agenda

The mass media can't really tell you what to think, but they may do a pretty good job of telling you what to think about. One week, the agenda-setters report on a study asserting that eating tree bark and prunes prevents colon cancer. The next week, they may report on a new study warning that too much tree bark promotes prematures psoriasis. Then the pack charges off on the scent of another story and never mentions tree bark again. Now you see it (and think and talk and perhaps worry about it); now you don't.

A writer must set her own agenda. She must name her days and herself. She must paint her skies and grass the way she believes them to be or the way they must be to make the story work. She must have the strength and tenacity to stick to a project in the face of the world's hostile or indifferent reception, even though to do so may make her appear foolish and childish and perhaps even insane in the eyes of the world. She must learn to say, "I am not you," and then to keep saying it, as often as necessary.

It may make her lonely, but it won't make her wrong.

Trusting Yourself

In a famous psychology experiment, graduate students at the University of Southern California were presented with a guest lecturer, introduced to them as "Dr. Wolff." The eminent authority spoke to them at length, and afterward the students filled out evaluation forms. Almost without exception, they professed to having been awed by the profundity of the pedant.

Then their professor told them that "Dr. Wolff" was in fact an actor, who had delivered a speech loaded with polysyllabic, Latinesque nonsense. He made no more sense than Dr. Irwin Corey or Casey Stengel.

The point? The students trusted the context more than their own intuitive reactions or observations. If their professor said the guy was an expert, then he was an expert, no matter what sort of rot came out of his mouth. And the students didn't even get mad at having been tricked and having their time wasted. In their view, the professor had the right to say and do whatever he wanted.

If only there had been a child in the audience to shout out, "The professor isn't wearing any clothes."

Before we get to feeling too superior to those college students, who were, after all, under a great deal of grade-pressure to conform, we'd better take a look at some of the authoritative messages we're asked to endorse every day.

Stumbling Through the Fog

Somebody sent me a brochure attempting to persuade me to spend my time and money on one of their seminars. Although the program presenters "come from different disciplines of thought and divergent areas of experience," the brochure assured me,

> each has found that the use of the written word in its utilitarian and creative expressions can provide an effective means of discerning problematical areas and foster corrective and remedial ideas which enhance movement toward greater personal free-

dom, an essential element for processing integrity and equilibrium.

Imagine how assured I was. After further review, I decided that the basic message boiled down to: "Writing can help you solve your problems." So why didn't they say so? Were they afraid I wouldn't be impressed if they made their pitch in clear, simple English? Did they really think that all that fog would make things look better to me? I probably don't need to tell you that I didn't sign up for the seminar.

Here's another bit of wisdom on the importance of clear writing, a hunk from a memo drafted (but certainly not crafted) by a school superintendent:

> It is necessary that schools and school districts emphasize the importance of imparting to students the skills and attitudes which are the underpinnings of a comfortable, confident, successful producer of all forms of written matter. . . .

Do you suppose he was trying to say, "Schools should teach students to write well"? If so, now we know why some schools aren't doing such a good job of it.

Lest you think I'm reaching far afield for examples of gobbledygook in daily life, pick up your tube of toothpaste and read the copy printed on it. I'll bet it promises that the wonderful goo you're now holding in your hand:

> . . . has been found to be an effective decay preventative dentifrice when used in a conscientiously applied program of oral hygiene and regular professional care.

Which means nothing more than that the stuff is pretty good toothpaste and will probably do you some good if you remember to brush your teeth and see your dentist.

Kids call it toothpaste. Only an adult would think to blow it up into "decay preventative dentifrice."

Seeking Validation

As we grow older, we learn to seek acceptance and advancement by embracing orthodoxy, expressed in the cant of the day. And we learn to look to others to validate our worth and to give us a reflection of our true selves. Students often ask me to evaluate their writing, which I'm pleased to do—although I always issue the caveat that they're getting one writer's opinion, not Holy Writ. But some then ask me if I think they have talent, if I think they can make it as writers, if I think they should even try.

I can't answer such questions. I don't think anybody can make such a judgment for anyone else. We each must look inside ourselves to see if we have the desire, the persistence and the courage we'll need.

Dancing With Rejection

Michael Blake wrote his novel while living in his car. Publisher after publisher rejected his work. Nobody wanted a Western, especially not one sympathetic to Indians. To survive, Blake took a job washing dishes in a Chinese restaurant in Bisbee, Arizona.

Finally, offers from two paperback publishers came through on the same day, and Blake's vision made it into print as a paperback original. The hardbound version, the screenplay and the Academy Award for *Dances With Wolves* came later, all because Blake held onto his belief in his project, even when the world didn't want it.

For every "overnight success" like Blake, there are dozens who never succeed. But that doesn't invalidate their effort or their vision.

Singing Memories

We must resist positive as well as negative judgments. Acceptance can be as corrosive as rejection, and we can become trapped in our successes.

Ozzie and Harriet Nelson's son Ricky was one of the first rock stars to wear the mantle of "teenage idol." He enjoyed great success with hits like "Hello, Mary Lou" and "Travelin' Man." But when he tried to move on to new types of music, fans insisted that he continue to sing the songs that had made him famous. When Nelson attempted to break away from the oldies during a Madison Square Garden rock revival, the fans began to boo. Although Nelson later learned that the boos were for security police and not for him, the experience lodged in his subconscious. Six months later, Nelson wrote his response in a song called "Garden Party." Since you won't be able to please everyone, Nelson sang, you must first please yourself. He'd rather drive a truck, he told his fans, than to sing only memories.

Ironically, the song revived his career for a while, but then the rocker, by now well into his forties, sank into relative obscurity before his death in a plane crash on New Year's Day, 1986.

Trying to Kill Off Holmes

James Goldman's story to the contrary, Sherlock Holmes died on May 4, 1891. Holmes and archfoe Professor Moriarty fought to the death in a tale titled "The Final Problem."

Holmes's creator, Sir Arthur Conan Doyle, had simply become tired of his popular creation and wanted to devote himself to writing historical novels, which he considered to be of more substance. And besides, he was running out of clever clues for Holmes to deduce.

From the moment they broke into print, in a story called "A Study in Scarlet" in the December 1887 issue of *Beeton's Christmas Annual*, Holmes and his sidekick and foil, Dr. John H. Watson, were enormously popular. Through twenty-four stories and two novels, Doyle fed the public's voracious appetite for Holmes's adventures. But Doyle yearned to do other, better things, and so on May 4, 1891, Doyle killed off Holmes.

Or tried to.

The public wouldn't have it. They wrote outraged letters to publishers. Young men went around London wearing black crepe in their hats and mourning bands on their arms.

Doyle kept Holmes dead for almost a decade, bringing him back in 1901 for "The Hound of the Baskervilles," which Doyle insisted was a reminiscence, not a resurrection. But new life for Holmes came in October of 1903, when publishers in England and America made Doyle an offer just too good to turn down.

"The Return of Sherlock Holmes" explained away the apparent death struggle at Reichenbach Falls. Holmes had slipped out of Moriarty's grip and spent the next ten years in Tibet. (As implausible as that may seem, the explanation went over far better than the attempts of writers for the TV prime-time soaper "Dallas" to toss off an entire year's episodes as simply a bad dream.)

Holmes lived on for thirty-two more stories and two more novels. Members of over three hundred organizations worldwide still study Holmes, and folks still write to Holmes at 221 B Baker Street. Most of us know him best through the Basil Rathbone portrayals in a series of movies in which Holmes was fond of uttering "Elementary, my dear Watson" — even though he never did so in the Doyle stories.

When we are successful, the pressure is strong to simply repeat the patterns that won us praise. We mustn't let the praise persuade us to repeat past accomplishments when it's time to take chances and try new projects.

The master writer reserves the right to make the final judgment about the worth of her work. She appreciates praise, but she doesn't live — or write — for it. She uses the judgments of others to inform and temper her own evaluation of her work, but nobody can tell her whether or not the projects she chooses are worth her time and energy, which are hers alone to spend. She doesn't look to the world to define her, based on what she has written; she defines herself as she writes.

Like a child anxious to tell her story, the master knows that her vision is unique and that her unique vision, honestly rendered, is her only gift to the world. She also knows that it is a great gift.

The master remains faithful to that vision even if she can find no one else to share it. To those who ask her to deny her truth, she says, "No! I am not you."

■ ■ ■ ■ ■ ■ ■ ■ ■ ■ ■ ■ ■ ■ ■ ■ ■ ■ ■ ■
Exploration: Finding
Yourself in Your Writing

 Spend ten minutes completing as many "I am" statements as you can. Begin each sentence with "I am" and let yourself finish any way you want to.

Set your statements aside for a bit. When you reread them, do any of them surprise you? Select a surprising statement, or simply an interesting one, and copy it at the top of a new page in your notebook. Spend ten minutes flow-writing based on this statement. In flow-writing, you keep the words coming without stopping, without thinking, without analyzing or evaluating. Just keep the pencil or pen moving.

This exploration can help you to define yourself, as a writer and as a person. It can also strengthen your writing "muscles" and get you into the healthy habit of converting your thoughts into words on paper. You'll be letting your child teach your master how to write with skill and insight.

Do your "I ams" and your flow-writing before reading on.

Avoiding Confrontation

I sat at a tiny table in the Steep & Brew Coffee House near my office one morning and scribbled a long list of "I ams." They ranged from the superficial through the silly to the obscure. Some contradicted others—"I am enthusiastic. I am cynical. . . . I am shadow. I am light." Some were whimsical—"I am the Midnight Coyote." "I am the Dawn Runner." Some strike me now as being worth thinking about—"I am all the I's I ever was."

I found the statement "I am a coward" nestled among my long list of self-assertions. It surprised me, and so I chose to write about it. This is what came out.

> I saw the young man slip the silverware into the inside pocket of his jacket.
>
> He had eaten our food. He had let us serve him. And now he was stealing from us—and from all the others who come to us for food, shelter and companionship.
>
> Did he hate us for seeing his need exposed?
>
> I saw him take the silverware, and I felt a surge of anger and outrage. I also felt afraid. What would he do if I confronted him? I hesitated, unable to decide what to do. He strutted across the church basement-turned-dining room, aware that his friends had seen what he had done and were watching him. He turned the corner and was gone.
>
> I did nothing.
>
> Later that day, when I thought about that moment, I imagined myself stopping him, even fighting with him. But at the moment, I had been paralyzed. I was silent. I was a coward.

Here's another writing, triggered by the notation, "I am an ex-smoker."

Kicking the Weed

Friends don't believe it when I tell them.

> "You? You used to smoke?"

The old health nut, exercise freak, eater of oat-bran, designated driver to the world?

> "Camel nonfilters, the real hard stuff."

Late at night in the frat house. Five-card draw and seven-card stud. More money in the pot than most of us can afford to lose.

"Got a cigarette?"

"Yeah, I got a cigarette."

"Can I borrow one?"

"Borrow?"

"I thought you quit."

"He didn't quit smoking. He just quit buying."

"I suppose you need a light, too."

"If you wouldn't mind."

"It's to you, McAdams."

"Hold your horses."

"Are you in or out?"

McAdams squints through the smoke, perhaps hoping his cards will have changed their spots since he last looked.

"I'm out," he says with a sigh.

Poker without a cigarette? Unthinkable. Cigarettes with coffee. Cigarettes after food. Cigarettes while writing deep into the night. A pack of cigarettes in the breast pocket of my Army fatigue jacket, as much a part of my uniform as my torn jeans and T-shirt.

The last cigarette came just before a long run in the Arizona desert. Got to beat my older brother, who acts as if he invented jogging. I'll show him. I'll burn him. I burned him, and every cigarette I ever smoked came back to choke me. I finally had to make up my mind. No more cigarettes.

Twenty years later, I still get smoking dreams and wake up feeling guilty. I stopped smoking them. I never stopped wanting them.

2

Starting From Scratch

It began with Shredded Wheat, crayons and a stapler in the
Brandywine freight office of the Reading Railroad.
—*Jack Rowe*

Kids don't know how to do things the right way, so they make up
their own ways.

Watch a pack of boys and girls playing pick-up softball in the
local park. The first batter has his hands crossed on the handle of
the bat. The second clutches the stick with her hands five inches
apart. The third holds the bat high overhead like a club. (He also
sticks out his tongue and chews on it in concentration, but that's
another matter.)

The rules adapt to the circumstances. A ball hit over the fence is
an automatic out because it takes so long to retrieve the ball. If the
right fielder has to go home, anything hit to the right of Willie's
shirt is a foul ball. Each team has to provide its own catcher, so
there's no stealing allowed. When the game dwindles to just three
or four to a side, anything over the "line" between second and third
base becomes a hit, and the fielder only has to throw the ball to the
pitcher to stop the advance of the runners.

The game goes on for hours, through heat so punishing the black-
top melts underfoot, through a sudden thunderstorm, through
twilight and until long past sundown. Nobody watches. Nobody
keeps score. Nobody coaches the players. The kids just play for the
fun of it.

When those kids get a little older, adults may provide them with
well-kept playing fields, fancy uniforms (with the names of local

business sponsors printed on front and back, turning the kids into walking billboards) and official rules. But with all the big-league trappings comes big-league pressure to perform. Coaches berate players who fail to "execute." The parents scream even louder than the coaches.

Soon the peewee league players may mimic more than their major league heroes' mannerisms at the plate and on the mound. Some get pregame stomachaches and postgame depressions, just like the big guys. And they may carry their alleged failures with them for life.

Maybe those sloppy pickup games weren't so bad after all.

Solving Problems With Fantasy

As a child, you probably engaged in endless fantasies. Your body may have been trapped in the here and now, but your mind could roam through time and space. The distinction between "real" and "make-believe" didn't mean a whole lot back then.

If you had a problem, you made up a solution. Having trouble with the gang from the next block? "Let's build a great big fort and dig a moat around it and get some alligators and put them in the moat. . . ."

You didn't know enough to know that your solution couldn't work. Okay, you didn't happen to have any actual alligators to put in the trench you hadn't actually dug yet. But Edison didn't have any filament, either. All he had was an idea for something called a light bulb. (Did a little candle light up over his head when he got this big inspiration? Just wondering.)

As we grow up, most of us learn to focus on a narrow band of "practical" solutions and to pay attention to only those experiences directly relevant to school, family and job. We suppress the rich fantasy life inside us and, with it, our willingness to posit wild dream solutions to problems. We stick to the possible and the proven.

We borrow others' solutions — because they seem to work for others, because it's safe to do as others have done, because we're under too much pressure to gamble on something new. We use the solutions we used yesterday, because they worked for us yesterday, because we didn't get in trouble, because we don't want to take the time to invent it all again today.

In settling for old solutions, we cut ourselves off from our creativity and originality, powerful tools for making better solutions.

Can you think of specific occasions, within the last twenty-four hours, when you've done something simply because "That's the way it's done" or "That's the way I did it before"? Think about getting up in the morning and then walk yourself through a typical day. Take a few minutes to list a few of the problems you solve on automatic pilot.

You could probably come up with hundreds. From tying your shoes and brushing your teeth to putting milk on the granola and washing the bowl when you're finished, from driving your car or riding your bike to booting up the word processor or inserting paper into the typewriter carriage — your day is filled with rote actions — things done the same way you did them last time, the same way you'll do them next time.

And that's not bad. You don't want to give a lot of thought to these simple tasks. Routines are necessary and can be sustaining, especially on the bad days.

We do much of our writing by rote, too, automatically making a verb conform to its subject and a pronoun to its antecedent, for example. We don't have to reinvent grammar and syntax every time we write. This foundation enables us to focus our attention on the more challenging issues in writing a magazine article or a sonnet or a short story.

But we mustn't remain on automatic pilot when we reach for the best way to translate our visions into words and to get what's in our heads and hearts onto paper and, ultimately, into the reader's head and heart. Such challenges demand that we let go of yesterday's solutions, ours and others'. The master writer builds on the wisdom of those who have gone before. She uses routine and structure to sustain and support her in her writing. But she also lets go of the "right way" so she can find *her* way. She may even return to a childlike state of fantasy to find the solutions her project must have.

Becoming a Water Molecule

Master boat-builders Peter and Olaf Harken of Pewaukee, Wisconsin, started from scratch. They scraped together enough money for materials and built their first boat in a garage.

"It was rough," Peter recalls. "In one of our first three years, our combined income was $3,800." But their love of sailing, a bit of business savvy and a gift for creative engineering enabled them to flourish as boat designers. Their worldwide reputation for excellence approaches legendary status.

Most boat-builders begin with what is. They practice the art of the possible, finding ways to make modest improvements on existing models. But when Peter and Olaf design a boat, they begin with "What if?" instead of what is. They defy all the "it can't be done" and "we've never done it that way before" naysayers and treat each problem as a creative challenge.

"There are two ways to go about it," Olaf explains. "You can engineer it to death, or you can just go ahead and do it and try it out. With totally unique shapes, it's usually easier to just do it."

"We try to visualize ourselves as water molecules, hurrying from the front to the back of the hull," Peter says. "And then we try to imagine the shape of the hull that will enable us to get from front to back the fastest."

As with designing a sleek, efficient hull, so with writing an evocative poem or a powerful suspense novel. The master writer builds and improves on existing structures, but she's also willing to start from scratch to create the new structure her unique vision must have.

What Next—Advertising in the Churches?

You may not like what Chris Whittle does, but you've got to admit that he's an original thinker.

Whittle is the creative force behind Whittle Communications. They're the good folks who brought us magazines that circulate only in doctors' waiting rooms and subsidized books that carry advertising. Whittle caused considerable stir in the educational community when he created Channel One, a newscast for secondary school classrooms, complete with ads for junk food and sneakers.

Is there any place Whittle wouldn't try to slip in an advertisement? In an article in the *New York Times Sunday Magazine*, he seemed to be seriously contemplating a way to get ads into churches.

Whittle recently unveiled plans for a string of for-profit franchise schools, kind of a McLearning concept, which he says will educate our kids better and at a lower cost per pupil.

Whittle doesn't just tinker with prevailing models. He looks for entirely new ways to deliver messages. No matter what else he may wind up teaching our kids, that would be a wonderful lesson for us all to grasp.

Applying structural chicken fat. Jim Stephenson is another visionary. As an engineer on the space shuttle Orbiter, he developed a number of techniques for solving problems creatively, approaching those problems from various angles.

He calls one such technique "subconscious brainstorming." He gives his design team a problem and tells them to go home and think about it over the weekend.

"The first response is, 'Yeah, right. I'm going skiing,' " Jim says.

But when they return on Monday, "you find that a tremendous number of new and innovative ideas have popped out" while folks were skiing or sleeping or doing anything but working on the project at hand, Jim reports.

"We planted the seed," he explains, "charged the people with the issue, defined the type answer needed, grouped the information, and let their subconscious do the rest."

To loosen up some of those brainstorming sessions, Jim says he'll often offer a crazy idea, such as using "structural chicken fat."

"The uninitiated look at me like I'm crazy," he says. "It shakes them up. Those familiar with my technique laugh and say, 'There goes Stephenson again. But he's right. We've got to open up our thinking.' "

The master writer gives her subconscious time to simmer a project and engages in her own creative brainstorming, allowing herself to think wild thoughts. She knows that most of those thoughts won't lead to usable words on paper. She also knows that a few crazy ideas will yield the insights and images her writing must have.

Becoming a traveler writing. There are lots of travel writers, and there are lots of writers who travel, but Chuck Woodbury may have invented a whole new category: traveler writer.

Woodbury publishes *Out West*, "the newspaper that roams." He drives the back roads of the western United States in his RV newsroom, writing stories about the museums, the diners, the campgrounds, and most of all, the people he encounters. He publishes the stories, along with his photographs and letters from like-minded readers, in his newspaper. Folks buy the paper, Woodbury puts the money back into gas and oil for the RV and toner for the laser printer, and off he goes again.

He began his odyssey in 1987, when he sold the weekly Murieta (California) *Times* but kept his Macintosh computer. That, a camera and a driver's license were all he needed to start a new business and a new life.

"At home, I don't feel like writing," Chuck told his readers, who now number in the thousands. "But once on the road, something snaps in my brain, and all of a sudden I'm passionate about it. Writing becomes like a drug to me. If I don't do it, I'm depressed. But when I'm writing, I'm as happy as I can be."

Nobody told Woodbury to do what he's doing. Nobody gave him permission to do it. He invented it, combining his two loves, writing and back roads meandering. He has literally taken his fantasy on the road.

If the form doesn't exist to accommodate her writing, the master writer invents the form as she writes.

Beginning With the Vision

I tend to read several books at once. My current bedside book is a novel by T.R. Pearson, the fine contemporary comic novelist. I've got a collection of columns by local writer George Hesselberg, *Paint Me Green and Call Me Fern*, in the upstairs bathroom. In the downstairs bathroom, I'm fighting off the Spanish with C.S. Forester's classic *Lieutenant Hornblower*. A Western called *The Day the Cowboys Quit*, by Elmer Kelton, keeps my mind off my pain while I ride the exercise bike in the basement. I'm carrying A.B. Guthrie, Jr.'s *A Field Guide to Writing Fiction* around with me in my backpack and pulling it out every time I have a few minutes.

These books are obviously very different from one another, but they have two important elements in common with each other and with every other novel, short story, play, poem, magazine article or limerick that exists. Each began as an idea, a vision, perhaps a fantasy in its author's mind. In each case, the author was willing to risk time, energy and perhaps agony on that vision, before anyone else knew or cared about it. She may have followed the vision in the hope of making money, or may have simply done it for fun. The vision itself may have been the impetus. Whatever the reason, the author did it.

Holding Nothing Back

So far we've forgotten the audience, the ones who may later read what we write. We mustn't allow ourselves to become so self-absorbed in our writing that we forget the folks on the other end of the process.

Children are sometimes so selfish as to be totally unaware of each other. But when they're with you, they're with you 100 percent. They're totally engaged—no holding back, no thinking about the next appointment. As adults, we learn to withhold, to defend, to impress. We fear negative judgment and so avoid revealing ourselves to others. We don't try too hard to be friends, because if we fail, it doesn't hurt so much.

Writers learn to withhold from their readers, too, and for all the same reasons. But to hold back is to stunt our writing, to make it less honest, less rich and textured, less quirky. The master writer holds nothing back. She lets all of herself into her writing, for the sake of the writing, and for the sake of the reader.

Writing to a pin-up. Noted author and adult educator Malcolm Knowles likes to tell his classes the story of how much trouble he had getting started on his master's thesis. He knew what he wanted to say but couldn't get the words to come.

His unblocking, he later wrote in *The Making of an Adult Educator*, marked "the turning point in my career as a writer."

"Who's the book for?" a friend asked. Knowles thought about that and named four people he thought might want to read his words later—his thesis director, a director of adult education, a university extension dean, and the director of volunteer training for the American Red Cross. At his friend's urging, Knowles wrote to the four and asked for their pictures, which he pinned up over his writing table.

"Is this clear and down to earth enough for you?" he would ask the face in one pin-up.

"Is this sophisticated enough?" he would ask another.

"All of a sudden, my fingers started racing," Knowles wrote later. The thesis, published in 1950 as *Informal Adult Education*, was the first of sixteen published books for Knowles, who, at last count, had also published 191 articles.

"I no longer write a book," Knowles insists. "I talk a book."

Entering into a covenant. Writers have all sorts of attitudes about their readers. Some give them no thought at all. Some condescend to them. Some simply say, "Take it or leave it."

Some court, entice, invite, bribe. "Come into my world," they say, "and I'll give you some candy."

Some treat the whole transaction like a business deal. "In exchange for a bit of your precious time and the momentary suspension of disbelief," the contract reads, "I will give you useful, or at least interesting, information, clearly and accurately rendered, or some sort of entertainment, or both." If either party reneges, the contract is rendered null and void.

The master writer enters into a covenant with her reader. She brings her whole self to her writing. She doesn't lie. In return, she asks that the reader bring her trust, her vulnerable soul, a heart capable of belief, a heart capable of breaking. The master writer would rather do anything than violate the reader's trust.

It's not a monologue, and it's not a transaction. The writing becomes a communion. How could the writer do any less than the best she's capable of? How could she hold back?

This is as true of a catalog description of plumbing fixtures as of a love sonnet. Everything the master writer creates for another to read receives her best effort.

■ ■ ■ ■ ■ ■ ■ ■ ■ ■ ■ ■ ■ ■ ■ ■ ■ ■

Exploration: Becoming the Cue Ball

 Think about an activity at which you are a master. Perhaps you're expert at baking bread. Somehow your loaves always seem to rise just right. Your crusts are crunchy and lightly browned, but the center of the loaf is moist and chewy and flavorful. Or maybe you have a gift for nurturing seeds into flowers. Others can use the same combination of soil, water, fertilizer and kind words uttered under cover of darkness, but your roses are somehow redder, your peonies more profuse, your lilacs livelier.

One of my college roommates was a pool hustler. We called him "The Iowa Kid," and he was the best I ever saw at sinking the eight ball in the corner pocket while leaving the cue ball in good shape on the nine ball. He was also a master at the psychological game. He knew when to speak and when to remain silent. "Don't miss," he'd murmur just as a skittish opponent was lining up a difficult shot. "Remember who's shooting next."

What's your forte? Spend a few minutes listing all the tasks you're good at, and then pick one for further exploration. Write a short explanation of how you perform the task. Don't research the project. Just write it the way you do it. You can frame the writing in the form of a "how to" article if you'd like.

Set the piece aside. Spend a few minutes forgetting what you know. Approach the subject as a child might. See it as a mystery. Fantasize about it. Become the milk in the bread (like Mickey in Maurice Sendak's *In the Night Kitchen*). Become the cue ball skimming across the felt. Become the water molecule gliding around the hull of the boat.

Now draw on your fantasy to write a second explanation of the process. Enter it from a different angle. Start in a new place. Be a different person.

When you fantasize in this way, you teach yourself two important truths about your writing.

1. There are no right answers, only possibilities.

2. It doesn't really matter where you start. Start anywhere, dig long enough, and you'll strike the core.

Don't look at your first writing until you've finished with the second. Set both aside for a bit, and then compare them. How is the second piece different from the first? Is it in any sense better?

Don't read on until you've finished your exploration.

Unaccustomed as I Am . . .

I've done a great deal of what qualifies as public speaking—as a college teacher, workshop leader and lecturer on the conference circuit—and have enjoyed generally enthusiastic responses from my audiences. I don't know if anyone else would judge me a master, but since we're learning to rely on our own evaluations of such things, I'll go ahead and call myself one, at least for the sake of this exploration.

Although I've become thoroughly comfortable standing in front of a crowd with my mouth in motion, I remember how nervous I was at first. And I've read the surveys that indicate that public speaking is a crippling phobia for a lot of folks. So, to help America get its butterflies flying in formation, I offer my mastery essay, written as one of my "kitchen table paper" journal entries.

How to Survive Giving a Speech

Provide! Provide! There's no substitute for preparation. Gather all the information you could possibly need or use and then gather some more. Anticipate the questions your audience might have.

Write out a rough draft. Think not only about what you want to say about what they want and need to hear.

Now rehearse. Talk into a recorder. Tell it to friends — or to the bathroom mirror.

Picture yourself giving the speech. Imagine it going exactly as you want it to go. In the theater of your mind, you are confident, witty and precise. Your audience hangs on every word.

Write a few key words on a notecard and then throw your other notes away. Don't read. Don't orate. Don't talk at or down to them. Talk to them.

Don't fight your nervousness. Welcome it. It's quite natural, perhaps universal. Harness this energy, using it to keep alert, in a heightened state of awareness and sensitivity to the subtle nuances of your audience's response.

Forget silly gimmicks like picturing audience members naked. Just remember, instead, that they really want you to succeed. They want you to be good. Pick out a few friendly, smiling faces and talk to them. Or, if you're feeling powerful and confident, pick out the man in the back, arms folded across his chest, a "says who?" look on his mug, and win him over with your logic, your humor and your passion.

Be yourself. Don't try to adopt mannerisms that work for someone else but that feel unnatural to you.

Don't forget to breathe! Draw air from deep down.

Take your time.

When you finish what you want to say, shut up.

Save time for questions, and don't be afraid to get them. "I don't know" is a perfectly acceptable answer. Listen carefully to the questions. They'll let you know what you really said.

That's the basic how-to, dredged up from my experience and from a bit of reading I've done on the subject.

Now here's a totally different approach, the product of another early morning "kitchen table paper" journal writing session in which I had an image of waves of energy beamed from the audience at the speaker.

The Zen of Public Speaking

Audience members bring their own energy, their own need. If you are an inattentive or self-absorbed speaker, speaking only what you need to say, with no regard for what they have come to hear, or if you are a frightened, defensive speaker, you will deflect these individual energies.

Some of that energy will turn inward, further isolating audience members in their fantasy, their boredom and their resentment. Others will turn their energy on you, and you will feel assaulted and not know why. You may become even more fearful or hostile, and all your worry will become a self-fulfilling prophecy.

Don't hide from the energy. Let yourself feel and respond to it. Coax and gently direct its flow, starting where it begins and blending the individual rills into a single, surging river. You will then become a part of the flow while still subtly directing it.

The audience becomes a single consciousness, flowing in a single direction, toward a single goal, the attainment of which becomes inevitable. They will feel this union and will become elated, although they won't know why. They may attribute the feeling to some mystical or heroic quality in you. They may rush forward to shake your hand afterwards, to take away something personal from you, a touch, a word, an autograph. But it is their own energy and wisdom they celebrate.

Each such encounter is unique and can never be duplicated. Allow it to be itself. Don't try to overcontrol it.

The first version is much more practical, useful and, I suspect, publishable. It's probably a lot more along the lines of what the reader is expecting to find under the heading "How to give a speech." But by letting myself float on the Energy River for a few minutes, I've gained a new way of looking at the interaction between speaker and audience. I can bring that new insight with me when I go back to revise the original how-to.

I happened to be speaking at a writer's conference the day after I wrote my "Zen" guide to flow management. The metaphor I had discovered made my talk a richer experience for me and, I dare to hope, for the members of my audience.

When you combine adult mastery with childlike fantasy, when

you step away from accepted forms, language and attitudes, exploring new ways of looking at reality, your writing gains perspective, authority and emotional intensity. Your reader will become absorbed in your words, will understand them in a new way, and feel their power.

3

Creating Something Out of Nothing

> There are three rules for writing a novel. Unfortunately,
> no one knows what they are.
> — *Somerset Maugham*

When you were a kid, you could make a toy out of just about any-thing. A pipe cleaner presented so many wonderful possibilities. You could twist it, bend it, put it in your mouth, curl it around your finger, push it along the floor (with appropriate putt-putt noises), fly it like a plane (accompanied by vroom-vrooms), load, aim and fire it, make it into a halo, a handcuff, a miniature hula-hoop.

But as you got older, you most likely learned that a pipe cleaner is for cleaning pipes — and nothing more. You gained knowledge but lost flexibility. Where once you could look at a pile of blocks and see a castle, now you see only a mess on the floor. The word "block" conjures up, not raw materials for building, but a mental barrier you hit when you start to worry too much about being a writer and not enough about the writing.

Ponder the Possibilities of the Pencil

Johnny Carson has a great routine in which he pretends to be a high-pressure television pitchman of the type prevalent in the 1950s. His product? The amazing "Dickie the Stick," which turns out to be nothing more than a plain wooden rod. Carson turns even the stick's plainness into a virtue — "You can paint it yourself!" — while extol-ling all the wonderful uses of "Dickie."

Like Carson and his stick, the master writer explores all the possibilities, even of the most mundane characteristics of her material, as she writes. Let's recapture a bit of your sense of the possibilities inherent in simple things. You probably have a graphite pencil close by. If so, pick it up now, and if not, imagine that you're holding the pencil. We use it for writing and for erasing, yes? How very grown-up of us. Now see the pencil through the eyes of the child inside you, who perhaps has no use for writing and erasing just now but can think of dozens of other uses for a slender stick with a rubbery bulb on one end and a sharp point on the other. Take five minutes to list all the uses you and your child can think of for this stick. Write them all down, no matter how silly. Let one idea suggest another.

Don't read on until you've made your list.

Presenting the Amazing "Paulie the Pencil"
Step right up, friends. Don't crowd. There's plenty for everybody. It's new. It's revolutionary. It's Paulie the Pencil. It's:
- A baseball bat for elves
- A rolling pin for making very small biscuits
- Something to bite on when you don't have a bullet handy
- A dueling sword
- A dog's fetch toy
- A cat distracter
- A back scratcher
- A hole puncher
- A button pusher (for those tiny calculators with the buttons too small for human fingers to use)
- A tool for resetting digital clocks
- An ear cleaner
- A belly button reamer
- Kindling
- The first log of a very small log cabin
- A propeller
- A splint for an elf
- A weight-lifting bar (for a very light workout)
- A flagpole for Fort Ant

Most of this is pretty silly stuff; you probably won't find too many usable ideas here. But the object isn't practicality. It's flexibility we're after. From this flexibility will come all the solutions you'll ever need to your real-life writing problems.

Comparing Apples and Oranges

At a recent workshop on writing advertising copy, my students and I got into a lively discussion of competitive advertising (Ray Charles says Diet Pepsi tastes better than Diet Coke; Burger King insists its flame-broiled burgers are better for you than McDonald's fried ones). I split the class into two groups for an exercise in childlike brainstorming, the sort of thing we just did with the pencil, only with a competitive twist.

To the first group I gave a fresh Washington State Red Delicious apple, to the second a Florida navel orange. I asked the first group to create a competitive ad trying to get orange-eaters to buy apples instead. To get them started, I had the group list all the ways their apple was better than the other group's orange. The second group had the opposite task. To convert apple-fanciers into consumers of oranges, they were to create a list extolling the orange over the apple.

Want to give it a try before reading on? Choose one or try both.

Why My Apple Is Better Than Your Orange
- You can eat the peel.
- You don't need a napkin.
- Paul Harvey eats one every day.
- An orange a day doesn't keep anything away.
- Apples crunch; oranges just squish.
- When you get done eating your apple, you can play "Apple core/Baltimore."
- Johnny Appleseed is an American hero; there's no Johnny Orange Peel.
- Apples are linked to romance: "Don't sit under the apple tree with anyone else but me. . . . You're the apple of my eye."
- You can bribe you teacher with an apple.
- Nobody ever shot an orange off his son's head.
- Nobody ever named a kind of computer after an orange.
- Apples are much more versatile than oranges. Nobody makes orange pie, orange sauce, orange pandowdy, orange Betty or hot orange cider.
- Apples are honest; you can always tell when an apple has gone bad. An orange is sneaky and will sometimes fool you into buying it even after it has gone rotten.
- Apples have lots of vitamin B and pectin. (The group wasn't really sure which vitamin apples have lots of, and they didn't

remember for sure just why pectin is good for you, but they were quite sure that it was.)
- Apples have lots of fiber, and fiber is better for you than anything.

Now Let's Hear It for the Orange
- They are wonderfully juicy.
- They taste better (obviously open to debate).
- Did you ever try vodka and apple juice? Yuck!
- They have vitamin C, which, according to Dr. Linus Pauling, will enable you to live darn near forever.
- They come with or without seeds; just try getting an apple without a core.
- They have their own protective, fully biodegradable package, so they don't bruise the way apples do.
- Every New Year's Day, two of the best college football teams in the country battle in the Orange Bowl. Who ever heard of the Apple Bowl?
- All our troubles started with that darn apple in the Garden of Eden. Oranges never did anybody any harm.

The Battle of the Fruits
I then asked each group to select one advantage and create an ad around it. Both groups came up with very sensual campaigns.

The apple group first thought to do a campaign on "The apple throughout history" or "Great moments in the history of the apple" but decided that didn't address the issue of superiority over the orange directly. So they centered their ad on that deeply satisfying crunch you get when you bite into a crisp, fresh apple, as opposed to the messy squish of the orange.

Ironically, the orange group made the squish their prime virtue. They created a huge picture of an orange with the juice spraying out in all directions and the headline "Just try that with an apple!"

What did all this accomplish, beyond getting everybody awake and involved and having fun right after lunch (no mean achievement)? It got all of us to put aside preconceived notions. (Who says you can't compare apples and oranges?) It helped us to think fresh thoughts, to explore new possibilities, to see commonplace realities in uncommon ways. That sort of unconventional, unfettered exploration leads the master writer to new insights and sharper, clearer ways to phrase those insights.

Leaving the Car at Home

As I write these words, Madison, Wisconsin, is observing "Bike to Work or School Day." The idea is to encourage people to use the bike for transportation, which means less pollution, less congestion on the roads, fewer fights over scarce parking spaces, less dependence on OPEC, and some good aerobic exercise in the bargain. According to the newspaper, about 8 percent of Madisonians bike to work in the summer regularly, and the city gurus would like to up that number.

I bike to work every day in good weather. Most of my commute is along a beautiful lake path, where I greet the emergence of families of ducks in the early spring and the formation of the first ice sheets in the late fall. In the winter I often walk, occasionally hitch a ride with my wife, and, on very rare occasions, take a car myself (and feel guilty—warm and comfortable, but guilty).

I suspect that most folks don't give a lot of thought to how they get to work. It's another of those rote tasks we do each day, and it takes something like "Bike to Work Day" to make us aware of what we're doing.

How about you? Is your commute or your errand route pretty well established? How many other means could you use and how many other routes could you take? Take a few minutes to brainstorm as many combinations as you can think of. Don't limit yourself to the practical or even the possible. Evaluating comes later. Put down anything that comes to mind.

If you put the means in one column and the routes in another, you can form dozens of solutions by combining an item from Column A with one from Column B.

How Many Ways to Work?

Column A: means	*Column B: routes*
cycle (bi, uni, tri?)	lake path
car	University Avenue
walk	through Univ. Heights

jog
hitchhike
bum ride with family member
taxi
stretch limo
roller blades (I could learn.)
snow skis (obviously seasonal)
bus (several lines to choose
   from)
rickshaw (Okay, I'm getting a
   little silly.)
private jet (Okay, I'm *really*
   reaching.)

via Regent Street
through Shorewood Hills

Even discounting rickshaw and jet as options, I've developed eleven ways and five routes, fifty-five options in about three minutes.

The master writer brings this sort of childlike flexibility to her writing. She ignores limits and sees instead the possibilities in a scene, an image, a word. She puts two characters together and lets them react to each other. She tries new angles, new combinations, new points of view. (Perhaps she'll have a character take a rickshaw to work.)

Master writer and teacher Ellen Hunnicutt puts it this way: "If you only write the story that is planned, you will miss the story that is revealed."

Alternate Endings: "The Revenge of the Wolf," or "Red Riding Hood Gets Hers"

You've finally got that little light of your life tucked and watered, and it's time for the nightly ritual of the bedtime story. You pick an old standard, one you haven't heard since you were a tyke. You plow through all that stuff about the basket of goodies and the path to Grandma's house in great shape. And then you get to the part about "what big teeth you have" and "the better to eat you with," and you remember that down the road the woodsman is going to chop the wolf's stomach open.

You hesitate. You hadn't remembered all that violent stuff being in there. Those wide, trusting eyes are staring up at you from the bed. Do you read on and risk nightmares? Do you mumble a lame

"To be continued," and risk having a very wide-awake, irate child on your hands? Or do you make up your own, nonviolent ending?

If you choose the last option, how many ways could you end the story of "Little Red Riding Hood" from the point when Red confronts the wolf in Granny's clothing?

Take a few moments to consider alternatives.

Here are a few possibilities:

• Wolf eats basket of goodies (which included a mild sedative to help Granny sleep, what with her arthritis and her nervous condition and all) and falls asleep. Red finds Granny bound and gagged but otherwise unharmed in the wine cellar.

• Red has been studying Kung Fu for several years, having been thoroughly versed in the dangers of assault and date rape. When the wolf makes his move, Red makes short work of him. She courageously presses charges and testifies in court. All the tabloids carry the story, with pics and lurid headlines. The wolf gets ten years to life in a medium-security prison.

• Red reasons with the wolf. "If you eat me now," she tells him, "you'll just get hungry again later, but you'll carry the burden of guilt with you always. Instead, why not change your ways, get a decent job, and save up for that little home in the woods you've always wanted?" Wolf pledges to reform.

• Take your pick on this one:
  1. A roving band of Teenage Mutant Ninja Turtles
  2. Batman and Robin
  3. A Los Angeles Police Department Squad Car or
  4. The starting lineup for the Oakland Athletics —
happens by just in time and:
  1. karate chops or
  2. batwhips the wolf into oblivion
  3. takes the wolf into custody without a struggle or
  4. touches the wolf for a three-run homer in the ninth.

You get the idea. There are many ways to end a story, even a "classic."

Trying to End "The Great Orange"

The late Dan Curley, editor of *Ascent* magazine, first taught me to play the "How many endings?" game. I wrote a short story titled "Le Gran Naranja" and submitted it to *Ascent*. The story grew from my family's cross-country move from California to Wisconsin in

1979. We caravaned in two cars, and at one point on the trip I began playing "What if?" (another fine game for writers). This particular "What if?" centered on my concern that wife Ellen and I not become separated for any reason. What if the husband glanced in the rearview mirror, and his wife were no longer following in the second car?

When I got around to writing a story based on my musings, I moved the setting from the Utah desert, where the idea occurred to me, to the mountains outside Santa Cruz, California (don't know why; just seemed more interesting), created the tiny hill town of "Le Gran Naranja" (don't know why there would be a town in Northern California named "The Big Orange" in Spanish, but that seemed right to me at the time, too) and gave it a sheriff, a commune and other bits of local color.

Dan was kind enough to write back to tell me that he liked the story but didn't like the ending. He said he'd be glad to take a look at a rewrite. Fortunately, I was just far enough along in my journey as a writer to know that editors don't say such things unless they mean them and that it's often wise to follow up on such encouragement. I hadn't much liked the ending either (I honestly can't even remember what it was), and I very much wanted to publish in *Ascent*, which was and is a fine literary magazine. So I set about refinishing the story.

Another version shipped off, another personal response, same result: good story, but the ending still didn't work for Dan Curley.

Or for me. I've never been especially good at endings, as a writer or as a reader. I often remember vividly everything about a novel I've read and enjoyed except how it ended.

I sat down with the story again, and only then, after several initial revisions and the second try with Dan Curley, a satisfying ending emerged. As soon as I got it, this ending seemed inevitable and right.

Want to take a minute to play "How many endings?" with my story before I tell you how I ended it the last time?

The case of the missing wife. Here are a few:

• She has car trouble, pulls off, gets towed into town, is ultimately reunited with husband and son (could be suspenseful or comic or both, depending on treatment);

• Submitted for your approval . . . the little warning light on the dash tells her to "Check Engine." She tries to signal her husband, who is singing along with Del Shannon's "Runaway" on the radio

and doesn't hear her horn honking. She takes the next off-ramp and
gets lost

> trying to find the elusive "Le Gran Naranja,"
> which turns out to be a ghost town,
> full of aliens disguised as humans,
> who arrived in a huge flying saucer that happens to look exactly
> like a
> giant navel orange,
> and the aliens abduct her,
> and the husband never sees her again . . .

Whoa.

• She gets kidnapped, all right, but not by aliens. She falls in with
a band of hill hippies, who decide to hold her for ransom.

• No, no, no. These gentle flower children wouldn't kidnap anybody. They offer to help her with her car, and in the process, their
gentle ways win her over. She decides to join the commune.

• Get real. The wife doesn't get lost. She doesn't get kidnapped
or seduced (by aliens or hill hippies or anybody else). She has decided to dump her husband (we'll go back and plant some clues) and
selects an unorthodox way to do it. She just turns off and never
looks back.

I went with the last option, a rather wry twist on marital rela-
tions. The story turns on the husband's slow realization that the
wife's absence is willful. Dan accepted and published the story, and
it won a prize and attracted the attention of a literary agent. I've
been a devotee of the "How many endings?" system ever since.

I should hasten to add that wife Ellen and I made it all the way
to Wisconsin (along with the kid, the dog, the three cats, the two
Volkswagens and walkie-talkies to maintain communications) and
that we're still together these many years later. Like many works of
fiction, "Le Gran Naranja" began with reality but quickly spun off
into fantasy.

The "How many endings?" exercise increases your inherent
ability to explore possibilities, to let your mind roam the way a
child's mind does. But it's purposeful fantasy, keeping you loosely
tethered to the specific writing task you've set for it.

Taking One More "Last Shot"

For one glorious season, Ellen and I served as cocoaches for the
Siena High School (Napa, California) women's varsity and junior

varsity basketball teams. We often brought young Jeremiah along to practices, and he happily ignored the action on the court, entertaining himself with his toy cars on the long benches in the grandstand.

Back when my knees and I were a lot younger, I hung out in gyms, playing pick-up and city-league basketball.

A combination of these experiences served as the seed for a short story I wrote and titled "Parting Shot." Morty Sklar published the story in a fiction anthology called *Here's the Story: Fiction With Heart* (The Spirit That Moves Us Press).

There's not much of a plot: A dad takes his young son to watch him play in a city-league basketball game. The dad doesn't play well; the kid doesn't much care. I tell the story from the point of view of the boy, who is unaware of his father's disappointment and perhaps even shame over his poor performance, unaware, too, that the father is at the age where he must soon consider finding less physically challenging pursuits (like changing the stations on the television with the remote control).

After the game, the father lets his son take a few shots at the basket, and then the father tries one last jumper. Perhaps he will use the shot as an omen or indicator: Make it and continue to struggle against the ravages of age; miss and hang up the sneakers. The boy is unaware of this possible level of meaning, but perhaps the reader considers it.

The man misses the shot. The boy encourages him to try again. The dad says, "Nope. That was it." End of story. It isn't *War and Peace*, but I hope I captured a small turning point in a man's life.

I began with the image of the dad playing and the kid in the stands. I didn't know how the story would end until I got to the ending. I didn't know about the "How many endings?" game when I wrote the piece, and since Morty was kind enough to accept the story as submitted, I never tried to come up with alternative endings.

I'm going to try now. If you'd like, take a few minutes to brainstorm other endings for my little story of a man, a boy and a basketball.

If you're ready, here are a few of mine.

Star player discovered in city league. The dad has the biggest night of his life, sinking graceful jump shots from all over the court and knifing to the hoop for drive after slashing drive. The boy is awestruck. By coincidence, a scout for the Boston Celtics happens to be in the stands and offers the dad a tryout.

"It just goes to show you, son," the dad tells his boy, "that anything can happen in this great country of ours if you just keep trying."

File this under Fantasy: Wishful-thinking Department.

Dad tries to push son into career he never had. Dad is a has-been or a never-was basketball player, still trying to find fulfillment on the court. He drags his son along to get the kid interested, but the kid wants no part of it (has his heart set instead on being an interior decorator/mortician/bank manager). Dad forces the kid to stay after the game and practice shooting until he makes one from the free-throw line. Kid finally makes the "parting shot." Reader draws own conclusions about what a lousy father the frustrated jock is.

Original story, but the last shot drops. Dad has lousy game, but makes the final "parting shot."

- He decides to hang it up anyway.
- He decides to give it one more try next week.
- Reader doesn't know for sure what he decides (the ever-popular indeterminate ending).

As for the boy,

- He's impressed by his pop (and gives up his own career notions).
- He didn't really much notice.
- He's much more concerned about getting home in time to watch "The Simpsons."

(Notice that we're beginning to play multiple endings within multiple endings. There are so many possibilities.)

Dad abducted by aliens. Whoops. Never mind. That must have seeped over from the *National Enquirer* ending I played with for "Le Gran Naranja."

■ ■ ■ ■ ■ ■ ■ ■ ■ ■ ■ ■ ■ ■ ■ ■ ■ ■ ■ ■

Exploration: Playing "How Many Endings?"

 Select a finished story—your own or somebody else's—and play the "How many endings?" game with it. How many different ways could you end that story? Don't judge, analyze or otherwise evaluate your endings as you jot them down. And don't bother polishing the prose. Just capture all the ideas. When you think you can't think of anymore endings, think of one more.

Set your list aside. Come back to it later and read it over. Do any of your endings surprise you? Where did they come from? Did you come up with an ending you like better than the original? Why do you prefer it? Do you have a good ending that demands a new story to lead up to it? If so, why not write that story now?

4

Naming the Possibilities

The limits of my language mean the limits of my world.
— *Ludwig Wittgenstein*

Eventually you got over the "No!" Mania (much to your parents' relief) and plunged directly into the Naming Frenzy — which may have been even more annoying to parents and other target adults. As your vocabulary began to expand to embrace the world around you, you needed to know the name for everything. You would accept nothing that didn't come with a label.

You soon learned that things have not one but many handles. That furry, slightly domesticated critter that slinks around the house and sleeps on top of the water heater has a generic name, *cat*, but also may be called *kitty*, *kitten*, *feline* or *tabby* (not to mention what your Dad called her when he tripped over her). And your cat also has a proper name, maybe Fluffy or Felix, Frank or Fydor.

Labeling isn't limited to the "right" names, either. One of Jeremiah's cats is named Maxwell. We call him "Max," which makes sense, but I also call him "Midnight," "Big Guy," "Hulk" and several other names totally unrelated to "Maxwell." After much deliberation, consultation and list-making, Ellen named her miniature schnauzer "Rosie." But most often she calls her "Boo Boo," and I usually call her "Bear." I don't know why, and neither does Ellen. We just do.

About the time you thought you had mastered *cat*, some grown-up warned you not to "let the cat out of the bag." Being unsophisticated as to idiom, you got confused all over again, trying to figure out who put the cat into the bag, where the bag was, and why you shouldn't let the poor cat out as soon as possible.

If your confusion left you speechless, an adult may have asked, "What's the matter? Cat got your tongue?" What a horrible picture that calls up in a literal mind.

Despite the chaos and confusion inherent in the naming process, you conquered *cat* and all its variations. With this mastery came a wonderful sense of power. To name was in some sense to control. If you could name the cat, you could understand "cat" and think "cat" thoughts.

At the same time, you were learning other related clusters of words. You associated *dog* with the critter itself and with *pooch*, *hound*, *mutt* and *canine*, Rex, Rover, Rosie and Rastafarian. You learned about a dog's life and dog days, about dogging it at work, and bull-dogging a project.

When Is a Drinking Fountain Not a Drinking Fountain?

If you move from one region of the country to another, you must learn a whole new lingo.

A few years back, Howard Mohr wrote a book titled *How to Talk Minnesotan*. You might remember Mohr as one of the writers and performers on the old "Prairie Home Companion" radio show. There and in his book, Mohr tried to teach us how to speak like a native Minnesotan.

You can't go far wrong, Mohr assures us, by answering almost every query with "You bet" or "It could be worse." Minnesotan food falls into one of three categories, according to Mohr. If it isn't a molded salad or a "hotdish," such as "Turkey Weiner Doodah Hotdish," it's lutefisk, which Mohr defines as "a translucent, rubbery food product with a profound odor."

Like all effective humor, Mohr's teasing is based on accurate observation. Minnesotans *do* talk—and think and act—a little bit differently than folks from other regions. And so do folks from New Mexico, Mississippi and Massachusetts.

When my family moved from California to Wisconsin, we encountered a whole slew of strange words for familiar realities. We no longer used a drinking fountain, for example. In Wisconsin, it's called a "bubbler." In Kansas and Oklahoma, your home probably comes with a "cyclone cellar." In California, we had no cyclones, and, for that matter, no cellars, either. In Wisconsin we have a basement, in which we huddle every time we hear the mournful wailing of the tornado warning siren.

Harping—and Swapping Wheelers—at the Local Gorm Sale

On rare occasions, regional dialect develops into something approaching a separate language.

Explore the twisting country roads of the Anderson Valley of Northern California, and you'll come upon the little town of Boonville. Everything seems normal enough, except that the coffee shop is called the "Horn of Zeese," and what looks to be a pay phone is labeled instead "buckey Walter."

You've encountered "Boontling," a language of some 1,000 words that developed between 1880 and 1920 and which is still spoken by a few older residents of Boonville—and by nobody else.

Residents borrowed words from the Pomo Indians and Spaniards who once lived in the area, shortened familiar English words (turning whiskey into "skee" and tobacco into "tobe," for example) and developed jargon based on local people and incidents.

For example, an apron is a "mossy" in Boontling, apparently because a cook named Mossy used to wear his apron all the time. When a local bartender tore off his mossy and threw it across the room, causing it to float to the floor, quitting your job became "butterflying the mossy" in Boontling.

Engaging in sexual intercourse is "burlapping" in those parts, allegedly because a store clerk and a young woman were caught making love on a bale of burlap bags in the storeroom.

If you want to learn more about Boontling, hunt up a book called *Boontling: An American Lingo*, by Charles C. Adams (Mountain House Press). Adams wrote the book twenty years ago, but it has recently been reissued.

The heading of this subsection is Boontling for "talking—and swapping harmless lies—at the grocery store," by the way.

Good, Swell, Peachy Keen and Terrif' The English language, with some 450,000 active words to choose from (and another 700,000 on the inactive list), is rich with multiple possibilities for expressing the same idea. For example, consider the many ways we have of saying that something is "good" or that we like it. Spend a few minutes brainstorming all the ways we can express this basic idea.

Here are just a few of the possibilities:

• It's aces, the berries.

- It's a beaut, a corker, a daisy, a dandy, a dilly, a honey, a killer (or even a killer-diller), a knockout, a lulu, a peach, a rouser.
- It's bang-up, A-1, first-rate, A-number-one, famous, fabulous, fantastic, great, grand, wonderful, awesome, swell, super, terrific, nifty, sensational, magnificent, marvelous.
- It's perfecto or maybe even perfecta-mundo.
- It's Jim Dandy and jake.
- It's the cat's pajamas and the cat's meow.
- Hot stuff. Hubba hubba.
- It's heavy, outta-sight, far out, cool, boss, bitchin', too much, crazy, gone, *real* gone.
- It's bad, mean, nasty.
- It's keen, neat, neat-o.
- Or, as they might say in Minnesota, it could be worse.

Talkin' Baseball

Just as words and idioms spring up in certain areas of the country and then pollinate (carried by television waves, as often as not, these days), expressions spread from a hobby, game or occupation to take on general applications. Just look, for example, at all the terms from baseball that have migrated into everyday usage.

We speak of something good as being *big league* and something less than good as being *bush league*, from baseball's major and minor leagues. *Grandstander*, *rookie*, *bench warmer* and *bench jockey* all come from baseball, as do *goose egg* for no score and *rhubarb* for argument. (Actually, rhubarb had an earlier, even stranger variant meaning, from the theater. When a director wanted a crowd to make mob noises, he or she would instruct the extras to murmur "rhubarb" over and over.)

We can thank the great Brooklyn Dodger announcer Red Barber for the baseball usage of rhubarb, along with the introduction of *in the catbird seat* for "sitting pretty," the state of having it made.

Even the phrase *charley horse* comes from a baseball player with a distinctive walk, and the phrase *There's no joy in Mudville*, of course, derives from the Ernest Lawrence Thayer poem "Casey at the Bat."

Baseball has given us all of these common expressions:
- Keep your eye on the ball (for remaining alert)
- He's got something on the ball (for moxie or smarts)
- Way off base
- Get to first base

- Right off the bat
- Keep pitching
- Take a rain check
- Two strikes against him

and dozens more.

Talking Girl-Talk and Boy-Talk

Some experts now contend that girls and boys develop two entirely different sets of meaning for the same utterances, based on differences in the way members of the two genders approach relationships.

Deborah Tannen outlines the differences in her best-selling book, *You Just Don't Understand*. For example, when a husband complains about a tough day at the office, his wife is likely to offer sympathy and support, Tannen suggests. But when the situation is reversed, the husband is likely to offer suggestions on how to solve the problem.

The difficulty arises when the speaker wants or expects one response and gets the other, the wife wanting consolation, for example, and receiving, instead, a list. She may feel hurt and put down. The husband, thinking he has been helpful and supportive, will be bewildered by his wife's negative reation.

Developing Your Three Vocabularies

Despite all these variations and sources of confusion, you eventually gained mastery over thousands of words, not just *cat* but *catastrophe*, *cataract* and *catatonic* (and maybe even *catafalque*) and expressions like "sitting in the catbird seat" and "cat got your tongue," along with the grammar and syntax needed to string the words and phrases together into sense.

In the process, you developed three vocabularies. Since you learned (and continue to learn) most new words by hearing them, your *passive hearing vocabulary* is the largest of the three and includes all those words you recognize by ear.

Your *passive reading vocabulary* encompasses those words you can also recognize in print.

Words you feel comfortable using in your own speech and writing comprise your *active vocabulary*, the smallest of the three.

I Don't Know How to Spell It, Doc, but It's Killing Me

To illustrate the difference between passive reading and passive hearing vocabulary, consider the word *aneurysm*. You may not recognize the word when you see it printed. But if you could hear it, you might well have at least a general sense of its meaning.

Try it this way: AN-your-IZ-em. Now that you can "hear" it, you may recognize it as a serious medical condition. If that's the case, the word is a part of your passive hearing vocabulary but not your passive reading vocabulary.

If you know that an aneurysm involves a dangerous weakening of the wall of an artery, and if you feel comfortable saying so in public, the word has made its way into your active vocabulary, the words you actually use.

See Spot Eat the Thanksgiving Monkey

You can see why a kid taught to read with phonics has a big advantage over a kid taught with the "look-say" method. With phonics, the reader learns the sounds of letters and letter combinations ("when two vowels go walking, the first does the talking and says its own name," for example). When confronted with a new word, she'll grunt and groan her way through, but as soon as she can say the word correctly, she'll often know what it means.

With the look-say method, the kid must learn the exact configuration of a word by rote to be able to recognize it each time she encounters it. "Stories" in "readers" aim at getting two dozen target words in front of the kid as many times as possible: "Oh, look at Spot. See Spot run. Run, Spot, run. Funny, funny Spot." Awful, awful stories.

The teacher may offer memory helpers, such as "Remember that 'monkey' has a tail hanging down at the end." Fine for "monkey," but what happens when the kid hits "turkey"? It's about the same size, and it has a tail hanging down at the end.

Pontificating With Pusillanimous Phraseology

Whether you learned to read by look-say, phonics or some combination of the two, you've gained at least passive mastery over thousands of words. You may even have enhanced your vocabulary by taking a self-study course such as the popular *Thirty Days to a More Powerful Vocabulary* by Funk and Lewis. Trouble is, you can learn a word such as *pusillanimous*, but unless you use it at least occasionally, you'll probably forget it fairly quickly.

And if you do use it, folks are apt to look at you funny and figure you're putting on airs. Why use *pusillanimous*, when you have a solid generic equivalent, *cowardly*, and several slang words ("chicken" being one of the printable ones) that seem to work quite nicely?

A master picks her words to communicate, not to impress. Sure, she could write about a *conflagration*, but she'd rather her reader understood that she was talking about a fire.

But she'll still want to have words like "pusillanimous" and "conflagration" in her tool chest. Although she might not use such show-off words, one of her characters might. By putting such a word in a character's mouth, the master writer reveals much about that character.

Building Your Useful Vocabulary

You can expand your useful, usable vocabulary by reading widely on subjects you're interested in and taking note of the new words you encounter. A "useful" word will keep appearing, and it will defy your efforts to replace it with a synonym.

Just now I'm reading two authors who are teaching me a great deal about life and language. C.S. Forester's series of Hornblower novels deals with the English Navy in the days when sailors relied on the wind and their wits to keep the ship heading in the right direction. These taut adventure yarns are an education and a great vocabulary builder. I'm also reading Elmer Felton's historical novels of the American West, encountering new words with which to phrase new ideas.

Does Skin Sleep in a Dermatory?

A relatively quick way to build a useful working vocabulary involves mastering word parts, those prefixes, roots and suffixes that keep showing up in various combinations in dozens of words. If you know the meaning of the word part, you can often figure out the meaning of the words it appears in.

For example, if you know that *dorm* means *sleep*, then *dormitory* and *dormant* will hold no mystery for you. If *pseudo* is false and *nym* is name, then *pseudonym* is just a fancy word for alias. *Auto* (self) and *graph* (writing) combine to give us self-writing (signature). Add *bio* (life) and you get writing about one's own life, or *autobiography*.

Another word for writing, *script* combines with *pre* for the writing before (prescript) and with *post* for the writing after (postscript).

Hypo means *under*, and *derm* means *skin*, so a *hypodermic* needle goes — well, you know where it goes.

There's no such word as *pseudopod*, but if there were, it would have to mean "false foot." If you were afraid of feet, would we call you *podaphobic*? Is a bad skin rash a case of *psychoderm*?

Sometimes knowing the root parts of a word will also reveal its derivation and history. For example, *photo* (light) combines with *graph* (write) to produce a photograph, which is literally "writing with light" on a negative.

Many words have outgrown their historical roots. If you write with a typewriter or computer, the product is still called a *manuscript*, even though your hand (*manu*) may touch it only to take it out of the carriage or printer. And most manufactured products today are anything but made (*fac*) by hand.

Five Words to Thrill and Amaze Your Friends

No matter what other words you make your own as you master new words to write and think with, here are five words guaranteed to win you bets at cocktail parties and to help you fill in those last blanks on the crossword puzzle.

The plastic casing on the end of the shoelace that enables you to thread the laces is called an *aglet*. The metal hoop on a lampshade is a *harp*. The indentation on the bottom of a glass or bottle is called a *kick* or *punt*. And the stick the shoe salesperson uses to measure your foot is called a *Brannock device*.

For those everyday objects and occurrences that seem to have no words to describe them, you can always invent your own. Comedian Rich Hall has made a fine living doing just that. His word for those crazy nonwords? A *sniglet*.

Touching All the Bases

Although she knows a lot of words, the master writer is careful not to contract *synonymitis* (an inflammatory condition caused by too many synonyms). This sickness is every bit as dangerous as an aneurysm. Although it probably won't kill you, it may slay your reader.

Sportswriters seem especially susceptible to this disease. A slugger belts a *home run* in the first inning, and the scribe duly notes the event. The next batter duplicates the feat (the wind must be blowing out), and the writer, not wanting to repeat a word, scrambles for eloquent variation, coming up with *circuit clout*. The third homer becomes a *round-tripper*, the fourth a *four-bagger*, the fifth a *long ball*, *dinger* or *tater*. The batter "takes the pitcher downtown" and "touches all the bases." The poor reader heads for the showers.

Some journalists have a hard time avoiding synonymitis when they bump up against the universal verb of attribution, *said*. Fearful that the reader is going to begin tripping over all those "saids" littering the news story or feature, the writer may be tempted to begin substituting *stated*, *noted* or *related*. No high crimes here, but possibly a misdemeanor, unless the writer really wants the slightly different connotations these words carry with them.

If *stated* seems okay, the writer may open the lid on the synonym chest just a bit wider, reach in and drag out *opined*, which sounds silly, or *claimed*, which indicates that the speaker is a liar. The synonyms may come pouring out, ghastly concoctions like *pontificated* and *expostulated*. Flushed by the exertion of trying to keep up with all of these jawbreakers, the writer may even have her subjects "smiling" or "barking" words, a physical impossibility.

Fact is, the reader doesn't even notice all those "saids." They're invisible, which is just as it should be. The master writer saves the variants for those rare moments when she really needs them, for emphasis and precise meaning.

Using the Way a Word Feels

The master writer knows that there are no true synonyms. Two words may carry the same denotation or dictionary meaning, but they will possess different connotations, the emotional associations that become attached to words. A *house* is not a *home* is not a *residence*, *abode* or *domicile*. *Mother* doesn't feel as warm as *Mommy* or *Mama*. *Mom* inhabits a middle ground. *Slender* sounds like a compliment; *skinny* doesn't. *Pudgy* doesn't sound as harsh as *fat* or *obese*. *Alias* has underworld connotations. *Pseudonym* is much more respectable, and *pen name* is downright elevated. (Put it in French, *nom-de-plume*, and it sounds truly classy.)

You can run most concepts along the connotation spectrum:

I'm *assertive*, you're *forward*, she's *pushy*.

My child is *inquisitive*, your child is *bold*, her child is *bratty*.

My car is *pre-owned*, yours is *used*, Honest Charlie's is a *junker*.

The master selects her words with care, for what they mean and for how they feel.

Using the Way a Word Sounds

Listen to a bunch of kids playing jump rope. They don't just jump and count. They sing their play.

> Fudge, fudge, call the judge
> Mama's gonna have a baby.
> If it's a boy, we'll give it a toy.
> And if it's a girl, gonna give it a pearl.
> If it's twins, gonna give it pins.
> Send it up the escalator,
> Send it down the elevator.
> First floor — STOP.
> Second floor — STOP.
> Third floor, we do not stop, for
> RED
> HOT
> PEPPERS!

Kids play with the rhythm and the sound and the feel of their language. They invent new languages for fun, and so that adults can't understand them. Didn't you ever talk Pig Latin with your friends? Ure-say ou-yay id-day.

The master writer doesn't lose touch with language on a feeling level. Words taste good in her mouth. Savor the sound of the tribal name *Potawatami* (POT ah WAT ah me). Poetry. Same goes for the name of the Los Angeles Lakers' Yugoslavian center, *Vlade Divac* (VLAH day DEE vocks). Say *Myth of Sisyphus* (SIS uh fus) five times fast.

I'll use any pretext to work *Saskatoon* (sas kah TOON) into my writing. And isn't *voluptuous* (vo LUP chew us) a perfectly pleasing blend of sound and sense?

Sound and sense don't always meld so nicely. *Syphilitic* (Sif i LITT tic) has a lovely lilt, until you take the meaning into account.

The master writer listens to each word, choosing appropriately soft or harsh, harmonious or discordant sounds to match her meaning. And she crafts her word combinations to speed up or slow down her reader, choosing a tempo to help her create the response she seeks.

Getting the "Easy" Words Right

Although she's interested in learning new words, thus expanding her ability to think and to communicate, the master writer also takes great care to use the common, everyday words correctly. The words we think we know and thus take for granted are often the ones that trip us up. To illustrate, take this quick test of words we use (and perhaps misuse) all the time.

Pick the right word from each pair (or is that pear?)

1. The bicycle, (that/which) was left on the porch, was stolen.
2. He ran (farther/further) in ten minutes than I could run in a month.
3. New Airy Ale has (fewer/less) calories than our regular beer.
4. I'd rather do 'most anything (than/then) take a grammar test.
5. The poor duckling can't seem to find (its/it's) mother.

How'd you do? Let's take a look.

1. The commas are the cue. The bicycle, *which* just happened to be sitting on the porch at the time, was stolen. If you meant to say, "The bike that was on the porch and no other bike in the universe," you'd use "that" with no commas.

2. It's *farther*, which means physical distance. *Further* is figurative travel, as in "He can't go any further with this line of inquiry." (He's not really going anywhere in a physical sense.) I remember the difference with the sentence "He goes *far*ther in his *car*."

3. If you can count them, it's *fewer*. *Less* refers to a quality, as in "less filling."

4. *Than* is the word of comparison. *Then* refers to sequence of time: "First he stumbled, and then he fell."

5. In every other instance, we use an apostrophe to indicate possession (the waddle that belongs to the duck is the duck's waddle), but since *it's* has already been taken by the contraction of *it* and *is*, we use *its* to mean "belonging to it."

"He Threw His Mother From the Train a Kiss"

I woke one morning to a somber report on National Public Radio, a follow-up story on the 1989 earthquake in the San Francisco Bay Area. "The committee will have to prepare an estimate," the reporter informed me, "of how much it will cost to repair the damage by next Monday."

Wow, I thought in my half-sleeping state. It will cost a fortune to clean up all that damage by next Monday! I don't even think they can do it.

Of course they couldn't, and they didn't have to. They only had to prepare the estimate by next Monday. But by misplacing her adverbial prepositional phrase, the reporter said something else entirely.

The master writer makes sure she puts her words in the right order. She knows that it makes a difference. To illustrate, insert the word "only" into the following sentence: (Put it wherever you think it belongs.)

I hit him in the eye yesterday.

There's no right way to do this, of course. It all depends on what you mean to say.

"Only I hit him in the eye yesterday" means that you did the deed without an accomplice.

"I only hit him in the eye yesterday" indicates that you didn't do anything else to him.

"I hit only him" and nobody else.

"I hit him only in the eye," not the nose, chin or mouth.

"I hit him in the only eye," thus rendering him temporarily blind.

"I hit him in the eye only yesterday," although it seems like years ago.

"I hit him in the eye yesterday only"; I didn't hit him in the eye today or last week.

He's just an ordinary man. The master also takes geat care to use specific language when she wishes to convey specific meaning. She knows that failing to do so can result in miscommunication. To illustrate, read this description:

His average income affords him a comfortable living. He's middle-aged and of average height and weight. He admits to only one real vice; he's a moderate cigarette smoker.

Now answer these questions about the subject of the passage you just read:

1. How much money does he make per year?
2. How old is he?
3. How tall is he?
4. How much does he weigh?
5. How much does he smoke?

We don't know the answers to any of these. But a reader will fill in the blanks, inserting her understanding of "average income," "moderate smoker" and the rest. I've tried this test on my students, and I can assure you that estimates range widely. One person's "average" $35,000 yearly salary seems like poverty level to another, and a fortune to a third.

I no longer dare ask my undergraduate students what "middle-aged" means; I can't bear to hear their answers.

This isn't to say that the master writer renders a list of statistics with each description. Such writing would read like a catalog and fail to create a picture in the reader's mind:

> He makes $35,000 per year. He is 5′9″ and weighs 175 pounds. He is 38 years old and smokes a pack and a half of Virginia Slims each day.

But if it's worth mentioning, the master writer will be specific, rather than leaving it up to the reader to guess. She selects her details carefully and purposefully. Does it shape your perception and reaction to know that the man smoked Virginia Slims? What if he smoked Camel nonfilters instead?

When Words Collide

Having just made what I hope is a strong case for care and precision, let me now make a pitch for letting the words bump into each other once in a while.

The Reverend Spooner used to have frequent linguistic accidents, such as "Pardon, me, ma'am, but this pie is occupewed." In his honor we call such slips "Spoonerisms." Peter Sellers perfected the art of the Spoonerism in the *Pink Panther* movies. Sellers would try to say, "He murdered her in a fit of jealous rage" and come up with "rit of fealous jage" instead.

That great American philosopher, Popeye the Sailor Man, is noted for meaningless mistakes that just sound funny ("how rebarrasking") and also for the mistake that enriches the phrase ("ill repuke" for "ill repute").

Closely allied with such inversions is the malapropism (named after a character in a Sheridan play), the substitution of a word for its soundalike. Folks usually commit a malapropism while straining to sound smart. The comedian Norm Crosby specializes in malapropisms, substituting *thespian* for *lesbian*, for example, or *mastication* for *masturbation*. Carol O'Connor used the same kind of schtick in creating the role of Archie Bunker for the TV sitcom "All in the Family."

Listen to a little Roger Miller music or watch any of the old Marx Brothers movies to get a sense of how much fun word collisions can be. Or read some of the poetry of e.e. cummings, who invents language, throws it into a bowl, gives it a shake and pours out patterns like:

> with up so floating many bells down

The "WHATZIT?" puzzle, in many newspapers, adds a visual element, the sight pun, to the word play. What's a HOLI DAY? Taking the day off, of course. If you were the postmaster or mistress, would you know how to deliver a letter addressed simply:

> WOOD
> MIKE
> MASS

It goes to "Mike Underwood, Andover [and over] Mass."

We obviously try to avoid making foolish (and potentially quite embarrassing) slips in public. But in the privacy of your writing place, with just you and the computer screen or piece of paper, you might try generating a few intentional accidents, just to see what develops. Sound plus meaning plus accident can yield insight. For example, suppose you reach into the tool chest for *information* and come up, instead, with *inflammation*? Inflammation denotes infection. Can we be infected by information? To inflame is also to arouse to great passion. Doesn't information at times light a fire under our intellectual burner, inciting us to act or to seek more information?

What kind of a world would it be if women got *minstrel cramps*?

Taking the Metaphor Literally

Our language is full of a type of wordplay that has become so commonplace, we've forgotten what the game is really all about. We speak of a "sunrise," for example, as if the sun really rose, even though we know the term is a metaphor to describe what it looks like the sun is doing.

Taking metaphor literally can spark new ways of looking at and writing about the world, sometimes with comic results. When I was a Boy Scout, our Scoutmaster instructed us to bring a green stick to the cookout, so we could roast our marshmallows and hot dogs over the open fire. Most of us understood "green" to be a metaphor for "fresh," so we hunted up a twig that still had sap in it and thus would be unlikely to catch fire. But one poor tenderfoot brought a wooden rod which he had carefully painted green.

Such confusions force you to examine your words and the assumptions that underlie those words.

A Rose by Any Other Name Would Still Be Banned From Baseball

The master writer develops an immense store of words. They are her tools and the materials for her creations. She respects and treasures words. She keeps alive her childish naming frenzy, continuing to seek out new words and the writing power they give her. She constantly looks for new uses, meanings and connotations of words.

But she remains humble in her knowledge. Just because she knows the names of things doesn't mean she presumes to understand the realities they represent. She remains open to the mystery behind the words. She doesn't mistake her power over words for power over the realities they represent.

"It seems to be human nature to assume that the act of naming results in power over, or understanding of, the thing named," warns language expert Robert Potter in his fine book, *Making Sense*. "What's in a name? Usually nothing—unless we learn to look behind the label."

The master is also aware that other cultures have other ways of naming. We say *head* (and also *noggin, coconut* and *noodle* on the slang end of the scale, *cranium* on the stuffy side). But the French say *tête* (as in *mal a la tête* or "bad in the head" for headache), the Germans say *kopf* (as in *sheinkopf* or "shiny head" for bald) and the Spanish *cabasa* (as in *loco en la cabasa* for "crazy"). So is that lump on your shoulders somehow inherently "headish," or does it seem more "tête-like"? Depends on what word you were raised with.

The master writer also keeps in mind that our ways of naming define and limit our ability to see and describe reality. The human eye can discern some ten million shades of color, but the English language has "only" about 4,000 words for those shades, and we usually settle for some combination of the eleven basic terms. Some languages have only two basic color words. In time we may learn to see only what we can categorize and describe; without words, we can do neither.

"Man lives with the world around him ... exclusively as

language presents it," according to philosopher Wilhelm von Humboldt.

■■■■■■■■■■■■■■
Exploration: Going on a Word Search

 Find a new word each day for the next twenty-one days—words that help you to name and describe the realities you want to write about. You'll most likely find them by reading about subjects that interest you and reading writers who challenge you.

If you decide to welcome a new word into your active vocabulary, write it on one side of a notecard. Be sure to include the pronunciation along with the correct spelling. You won't use a word you can't pronounce, and if you don't use it, you'll lose it.

Write the definition on the other side of the card. Define the word in your own terms, not the dictionary's. In that way, you'll be sure you understand what you're writing, and you'll make the word and its meaning your own.

Keep your growing pile of notecards handy and go through them once or twice a day, quizzing yourself on pronunciations and definitions. As you master a word, discard its notecard.

At the same time, take one word a day that has become an old friend and find a new meaning, a new usage, a new connotation for that word. Working crossword puzzles is often good for this sort of thing, since it forces you not only to search for new words but also to examine other potential meanings for clue words.

Why trouble seems to come in bunches. To further enrich and enlarge your word mastery, search out the origins of some of the common words and phrases you use every day.

Why, for example, do we "let the cat out of the bag" (or "spill the beans") to reveal a secret? Turns out the former expression comes from the streets of London, where merchants used to sell pigs in bags called "pokes." Some venders would substitute alley cats for pigs. If you were foolish enough to purchase without checking first to make sure what you were getting, you would be said to have "bought a pig in a poke." But if you were wise and checked the merchandise, you would "let the cat out of the bag" and expose the deception.

In the course of taking this exploration with you, I discovered that "trouble" comes from the Latin *turba*, meaning "crowd." That makes sense when you think about the way reasonable people behave when they form a mob. I also learned that "nice" comes from the Latin *nescius*, meaning "ignorant."

Studying the literal meanings of words from other languages can be revealing and thought-provoking as well. For example, the word for *friend* in one American Indian dialect translates literally as "one who carries my sorrows on his back." What a beautiful sentiment, and what a marvelous testimony to the spirit of the people who created such a language.

From reading Elmer Felton's *The Wolf and the Buffalo*, I learned that the Comanche dialect carries no word for *Comanche*. They have words for other tribes and for Caucasians, but they refer to themselves simply as "The People."

This kind of exploration, fueled by a childish curiosity to find the names for things, can yield immense rewards for your emerging master writer. The search will help you to develop a larger active vocabulary and to get into the good habit of acquiring new words each day. It will help you develop your flexibility in exploring the full power of the words you already know. With this knowledge and flexibility will come greater possibilities for expression and discovery in your writing.

5

Asking "How Come?"

I am an author because I want to ask questions.
If I had all the answers, I'd be a politician.
— *Eugene Ionesco*

Just about the time the naming frenzy subsides, "how come?" fever takes hold. How come dogs bark? How come trees grow rings? How come I have to go to bed now? Kids never stop asking "how come?" (In one of Bill Cosby's early routines, he has a child asking, "Why is there air?" His answer: to blow up volleyballs.)

After a few weeks of constantly being asked "Why?" exasperated parents may find themselves yearning for the naming frenzy. And they may seek refuge in answers like "because" or "I said so."

Sad truth is, when we get to be adults, we have little time for those childish "how come?" questions. We get all wrapped up in "How much (will it cost me)?" and "How long (will it take)?"

We need to know how to drive a car but not how come the car goes when we push down on the accelerator. We need to know how to use a word processor but not how come the letters appear on the screen when we punch the keys. We need to know where the light switch is but not how come the light goes on when we flip that switch.

We don't need to know these "how comes," that is, until and unless we have to try to fix an engine, a word processor or a light fixture. Then the "how come?" may become an imperative. Then, and only then, do we search for an answer — or for a repair person who already knows how come.

But the master, like the child, constantly asks "how come?" in contexts that would seem to have no immediate or practical application. Her curiosity is insatiable. How come I dream? How come a heart attack hurts? How come we use green for go and red for stop? How come the extras in a mob scene murmur "rhubarb"?

Often the questions send her off on an inquiry that yields rich new topics for writing or details that make her writing more interesting and authentic. And even the totally impractical explorations leave her more knowledgeable, more aware, more open to the world around her. Each answered question seems to produce ten new, unanswered ones.

How Come There's No Ivy in the Ivy League?

George Hesselberg, reporter/writer for the *Wisconsin State Journal*, asks himself "how come?" questions all the time—and often ends up getting a column out of the answers.

For example, one day he was driving through the University of Wisconsin-Madison campus and happened upon a work crew tearing the ivy from the walls of the Old Science Hall, one of the oldest and most picturesque buildings on campus. George wondered "How come?"

He asked. And he kept asking until he found out. The ivy vines, it turns out, were getting into the cracks between the stones. If left untended, they would have gradually caused the venerable old building to crumble. Water would follow the tendrils into the cracks, freeze and expand, making more cracks. Pretty soon, there'd be more cracks than stones, and students would be conducting their lab experiments out on the icy slopes of Bascom Hill.

Being a true reporter, George went further. More "how come?" questions led him to the discovery that there's hardly any ivy left in the Ivy League, for the same reason.

■■■■■■■■■■■■■■■■■
Exploration: Asking
"How Come?"

 This entire chapter will be an exploration. Begin your search by making a list of "how come?" questions. You won't have to search far. Just take a look around you. Don't struggle for profundity. Simple questions are likely to be the best.

When you've thought of as many questions as you can, think of at least one more. Don't read on until you've finished your brainstorming.

Carry your notebook around with you for a week or so or for as long as you want. Every time a "how come?" question occurs to you, jot it down. As with your other explorations, don't judge, evaluate or analyze what you're writing. If a question occurs to you, simply note it. You may find that, as you begin to pay attention to these sorts of questions, more and more of them occur to you. They've probably been occurring to you all along. You just stopped paying attention.

After you've built a sturdy list of "how come?" questions, go back over your list and find a few you'd really like answered. Select one and find at least a tentative answer within the next day or two. Do as many questions as you'd like.

This exploration will reawaken and nurture your childlike curiosity and will also strengthen your resourcefulness in finding answers.

After you've finished at least the initial brainstorming part of this exploration, read on.

How Come Donuts Have Holes?

A recent series of beer commercials poses a number of "Why?" questions. "Why do women have the answers?" one series begins. The series inevitably ends with the question, "Why ask why?" The idea seems to be that we'd be better off simply guzzling beer, preferably the brand made by the creator of these ads. The unexamined life is just fine. Drink up.

I obviously don't agree with that philosophy. Asking "why?" is healthy, natural and fun. Even if it yields more questions than answers, and even if the lack of answers can be frustrating, as the ads suggest, the questioning helps you to advance on your journey as you become the master writer that is within you.

This One's For You, L.M. Boyd

I'll bet a fellow named L.M. Boyd agrees with me. He writes a column filled with the answers to "how come?" questions. I used to read him in the *San Francisco Chronicle* when I lived in the Napa Valley. None of the papers I read now carry his column, and I only get to read him when I buy a *San Francisco Chronaminer* (or is it *Exonicle*? The *Chronicle* merges with the *San Francisco Examiner* on Sundays) at my local Pic A Book Bookstore. I miss Boyd, so I'll dedicate this next section to him.

Here are some of the "How come?" questions I came up with as I wrote this chapter.

- How come dogs circle before they lie down?
- How come dogs bark?
- How come they don't get laryngitis from all that barking?
- How come cats purr?
- How come the keyboard on the typewriter is laid out in such an illogical manner ("a" struck by the weak little finger, for example, and "e" an awkward stretch for the middle finger)?
- How come "objects in mirror are closer than they appear"?
- How come a 2 × 4 doesn't really measure 2 inches by 4 inches?
- How come one side of aluminum foil is shiny and the other side is dull?
- How come we use red for stop, yellow for caution (or for "speed up," as some drivers interpret it), and green for go?
- And how come the red is always on the top, the yellow in the middle and the green on the bottom?
- How come your skin wrinkles when you stay in the bathtub or swimming pool too long?
- How come a curve ball curves?
- How come salmon come back to the same river for spawning, the swallows find their way back to Capistrano, and the buzzards return to Hinckley, Ohio, every year?
- How come we always milk cows from the right and mount horses from the left?
- How come the gentleman walks on the lady's left?
- How come the sun or moon looks so much bigger on the horizon?
- How come yawning is contagious?
- How come you can't tickle yourself?
- How come a left-handed person has a shorter life expectancy than does a right-hander?
- How come some men go bald?
- How come women don't?
- How come leaves turn colors in the fall?
- How come we always eat turkey at Thanksgiving? (Or the tra-

ditional Thanksgiving monkey if you're still having trouble sounding out words.)

- How come, when you jog, the wind adjusts so as to be always in your face?
- How come whatever is good for your lawn is death for your trees and vice versa?
- How come there's chocolate, if it's just going to make us fat, give us skin problems and kill the dog if she eats it?
- How come there are such things as labor pains, teething, gum disease, bad backs, bad knees, cancer, AIDS . . . ?
- How come otherwise mannerly, civilized people slurp their coffee and chew with their mouths open?
- How come you always hurt the one you love?
- How come women have to shave their legs and armpits?
- How come the account number on a credit card is so long?

Enough. I'm starting to feel like a cross between Andy Rooney and Job.

There are no answers for some of these questions. Others turn out to be the wrong questions (wrong in the sense that they won't yield the answers I really want). But I was able to untangle a few of life's mysteries and am happy to share a bit of my new wisdom with you. Two books were of particular help to me with this: David Feldman's *Why Do Clocks Run Clockwise and Other Imponderables* (Harper & Row, 1987) and *The Book of Answers*, Barbara Berliner (Prentice Hall, 1990). There are dozens of these sorts of books available in the library now, and if they fail you, that greatest of all writer's helpers, the reference librarian, can probably steer you in the right direction.

Tales of barking dogs and nursing kittens. The folks who claim to know don't seem to agree as to why a dog circles before it flops. Some say it's to mash down the grass (even though the dog now sleeps on your shag carpet, which is already plenty mashed). Others say it's a throwback to life in the wild, when the dog had to make sure no predators were nearby before risking a dognap. Pay your money and take your pick.

Sure, they bark to warn you that their sworn enemy, the postal person, is approaching, and they bark to tell you they need to go outside. (They'd *better*.) But sometimes they just seem to bark for the sake of barking. How come? Wolf cubs do the same thing, and a dog is apparently a classic case of arrested development, a wolf cub that never quite grew up because it has learned to depend on humans for survival.

I'm sure this information will make you feel much better when you're lying awake on a summer night, listening to the neighbor's dog yapping and wishing the darn thing would develop laryngitis.

They *do* get laryngitis, by the way, but not often. Their vocal cords have become a lot tougher than ours, probably because of all that barking.

How come cats purr? I'm still not sure, but they learn to do it as kittens, in response to their mother's purring as they nurse.

Now, the real question is, how come each kitten gets assigned to a particular spigot as they nurse? It's true, you know. Check it out next time Tabby drops a litter.

Unjamming the keys. That one about the typewriter really bothered me. You, too? The more I thought about it, the more I became convinced that you couldn't design a keyboard to be less conducive to speed and convenience.

Turns out, that's exactly what the inventor had in mind. Christopher Latham Sholes created the typewriter in Milwaukee, Wisconsin. It was a marvel for its time (1890s) but a poor piece of work by today's standards. If you got up any speed at all on the thing, the keys would jam. So they actually laid out the keyboard in its present configuration to slow the typist down and thus prevent jamming.

So how come they haven't redesigned it, especially now that we have those marvelous word processors that can keep up with the fastest typist alive? Efforts to rearrange the keyboard, like efforts to introduce simplified spelling, have met with great resistance, perhaps because folks who have had to master the silly keyboard as it is want to make sure that neophytes have to go through the same misery.

Watch out for that car! Why, in heaven's name, would car manufacturers make a rearview mirror that distorts distances, so that the car you think you have plenty of room to pass is actually right off your bumper? Sounds like a plot by the auto body shop owners of America.

And while we're at it, how come it's only the outside mirror on the passenger's side, and not the driver's side outside mirror, or the inside mirror, that distorts?

There's a reason, and the reason even makes a little sense. They make the passenger's side mirror convex, which means it curves slightly out rather than being flat or slightly indented or concave, to increase the range of vision it affords. That gets rid of most of the "blind spot" all drivers experience when trying to see behind them. But the increase in range extracts a price in distortion of depth perception. Thus, "objects in mirror are closer than they appear," but at least you can see them.

You'd probably better just keep looking over your right shoulder before you change lanes or make a turn, just like your driver's ed teacher told you.

Red light/green light. When I was growing up in Southern California, we had a fellow on local television who called himself Engineer Bill. Every afternoon, he instructed us to go get a nice, big glass of milk from the kitchen, hunker down in front of the TV with it, and gulp down the milk every time he said "Green light." But whenever Engineer Bill said "Red light," we were to stop drinking immediately! (Or suffer what dire consequence? I can't remember.)

Engineer Bill would of course get tricky, starting to say "Green light" and suddenly switching to "Red light," or saying "Red light" two or three times in a row or saying "Green light" and then saying "Red light" real fast.

Was it just me, or did this game result in a lot of milk getting tossed, snorted and spit all over the living room carpet?

Maybe Engineer Bill is the reason why I'm so interested in the red light/green light question. But I suspect that this "how come?" is of particular interest to me because I'm color blind. I'm not just your run-of-the-mill red/green complex color blind, mind you, but full-blown can't match socks, shirt and tie to save his life color blind, can't be an airline pilot or electrician color blind, can't tell the red from the yellow from the green of a traffic light color blind.

Salt Lake City, Utah and St. Paul, Minnesota both claim to have had the first traffic lights, but my source, Kane's *Famous First Facts* (H.W. Wilson), gives the honor to Cleveland, Ohio, August 5, 1914, at Euclid Avenue and East 105th Street. Turns out the selection of colors for the traffic signals is simply tradition, a carry-over from the railroad. They add a bit of orange to the red and a touch of blue to the green to help folks with red/green complex tell the difference. (Doesn't help me a bit.)

The standardized arrangement of red on top, yellow in the middle and green on the bottom is also designed to help color blind folk and does help me a lot—except at night, when I can't tell the location until I'm very close to the signal.

So how come some states now run the lights on the horizontal rather than the vertical? And how come the lights always seem to go against you when you're in a hurry? And how come the slow poke ahead of you always manages to catch the yellow, but you have to stop? And how come there's never a left-turn arrow when you really need one?

Three right answers to three wrong questions. Your skin doesn't exactly wrinkle when it gets soggy. The tougher skin on your extremities absorbs water and swells, which makes it fold over and look wrinkled.

The leaves don't really turn colors in the fall. Those beautiful reds and oranges and yellows were there all the time. But in the fall, photosynthesis shuts down, and the dominant green goes away, letting the other colors shine through for a bit before the leaves fall.

And here's a real myth buster: the pilgrims didn't eat turkey at the first Thanksgiving. In fact, there was a movement to make the turkey the national bird, and who would eat the national bird? The custom of eating turkey at the holidays came later.

Milk, mount and heel. Apparently, we milk cows from the right side simply because most milkers, along with most other folk, are right-handed. Milking from the right gives the milker more elbow room. The cow has no preference.

But it's the horse that dictates that we mount on the left. They like it that way, and some get pretty skittish if approached from the "wrong" side. I haven't found out how come, and I haven't found out how come we always heel dogs on our left.

The gent walks on the woman's left, not because she's heeling him, but because that's the outside or street side. In case a passing car should splash water, jump the curb or in any other way create a disturbance, the man will absorb the brunt of it.

But perhaps this element of chivalry, like holding doors and picking up checks, has become hopelessly old-fashioned.

Could you read that number again—slowly? Social security numbers are nine digits. That's enough to yield one billion possible combinations. Since there are still fewer than 250 million folks living in America, that would seem to be plenty of combinations to see us through.

So how come credit cards issue twenty-digit numbers, enough

to produce 100 quintillion possible combinations? Surely they aren't expecting to sign up 100 quintillion customers. And surely they aren't doing it just to aggravate us.

Turns out there's a good reason, which I discovered by reading William Poundstone's *Big Secrets* (William Morrow, 1983). Poundstone reveals the recipes for Kentucky Fried Chicken's spices and McDonald's secret sauce, by the way. They're both pretty disappointing, but the secret behind Coca-Cola might surprise you.

Here's the reason, as Poundstone explains it, for those incredibly long credit card numbers. Suppose you want to make a purchase or secure a room reservation by telephone. The nice person on the other end of the line will, of course, want your credit card number. You read it off slowly and carefully, but let's suppose she mishears or mistypes or just plain misses, and the number she enters is off by one. It could happen, or else why do we get all those wrong number calls on the telephone?

If there were only enough numbers to supply all card holders, then that wrong number would be somebody else's number, right? And that person would get charged for your weekend at Niagara Falls or your purchase of the five-album set of Slim Whitman's Greatest Hits. And you could wind up with a charge for somebody else's Roncomatic slicer/dicer on your bill at the end of the month.

But with 100 quintillion possible combinations, the odds of the misentered number actually belonging to somebody else are pretty slim. The computer will tell the operator that no such number exists, and she'll know to ask you to read the number again.

This also protects the system from folks calling in and giving a random number, hoping to guess a real number and thus charge a purchase to someone else's account.

Nonanswer Answers

As good as my resources were for answering my "how come?" questions, I couldn't always find an answer, and sometimes the answer I found didn't satisfy me.

I read up on hair follicles and male-pattern baldness, and I guess I understand baldness better now. But I'm not happy about it. I guess I didn't want to know "how come?" in the physical science sense. I wanted to know "how come?" in the cosmic-injustice-of-it-all sense (as in "How come *I* have to go bald?"). I still don't understand.

I also studied up on curve balls, which it turns out are closely related to airplane wings. I already knew the "how." To throw a curve ball, you grip the ball along rather than over the seams. Just as you deliver the ball, you snap your wrist (clockwise—if you snap it the other way, you'll be throwing a screwball), letting the ball roll over your index finger.

If you want to practice this at home, use a tennis ball, or better yet, a whiffle ball. With a little work, you can probably start breaking off some pretty wicked stuff. You'll also put a tremendous strain on your elbow, so go easy.

But why do the grip and the snap of the wrist make the ball curve? And why does the bulging design of an airplane wing enable it to lift the heavy metal tube it's attached to into the air? A guy named Bernoulli figured it out. In both cases, air has to travel farther around one half of the ball or wing than the other. (On a wing, you want to make sure it's the top half.) Since the two halves are traveling at the same rate of speed, the air has to go faster to go around the longer half, and that uneven speed creates lift.

I've known it since I took physics in high school. But I still don't understand, really understand how a curve ball curves or how an airplane flies. My head knows, but my heart doesn't buy it. And I'll probably never know how come Nolan Ryan can make a baseball move the way he does.

That leaves plenty of room for mystery. There are always more "how come?" questions. As long as you keep asking, keep searching, keep alive your childlike sense of wonder, you'll keep learning and growing, and that will keep you traveling on your journey toward mastery.

6

Asking Stupid Questions

Live the questions now. Perhaps you will then, gradually, without
noticing it, live along some distant day into the answer.
— *Rainer Marie Rilke*

Kids soon branch out from "What's that called?" and "How come?"
and start asking all sorts of other questions.

"Whatcha doin'?"

"What's that for?"

"How does it work?"

"Where does it go?"

"Can I try it?"

As with the "No!" Mania and the Naming Frenzy, this phase in
the child may be quite annoying to the adult. But the child, uncon-
cerned about the impression she's making, keeps asking, not to
annoy but simply because she wants to know. The answers she
receives tell her much about the world and about the adults giving
the answers.

How old were you when you stopped asking all those questions?
Somewhere along the line, you may have learned that you weren't
supposed to ask, that you were supposed to know all the answers
already, that the questions you were asking were "stupid" (meaning
that you were stupid for asking them).

What If the Students Got to Ask the Questions?

In school, teacher asked all the questions, and you were supposed to
give the answers, which you were supposed to have memorized,

either from a book or from what teacher told you. If you didn't give the right answer, you got in trouble.

You learned how to look like you knew the answers even when you didn't, because teacher seemed to call on you only when you looked confused. You certainly didn't ask questions, because to do so would reveal your ignorance and draw the wrath of the teacher and the derision of your fellow students—who laughed because they were as full of tension and confusion as you were.

Imagine a classroom where the kids get to ask all the questions. Picture yourself in such a classroom, with a favorite teacher standing in front of the room. (We'll come back to the favorite teacher in a later chapter, so tell your subconscious to hang on to the thought.) If things got reversed in this way, would school be better or worse for you? What questions would you ask? If you like, make a list right now of a few questions you wish somebody would answer for you.

"What Is This 'Off the Wall'?"

I teach bright, talented college upperclassmen in the journalism school of one of the finest public universities in the country, which means that I get to share a classroom with a bunch of expert bluffers. They've long since learned to keep their questions to themselves and to look as if they know everything. If I say something they don't understand, they write it down anyway and hope it makes more sense later or that they can look it up in a book someplace.

After a few class sessions, they begin to realize that our discussions aren't in any book, because we're making it up together as we go along. They also begin to realize that I really want them to ask questions. They realize it because I throw money at them when they do—quarters and dimes if I'm flush, nickels and pennies toward the end of the month. I also bring a "traveling trophy" to class: my Mickey and Minnie Mouse pen set, my Batman bank, my George Bush doggie chew toy, my Greensboro Hornets baseball cap, or some other treasure. When someone asks an especially good question, they get to keep the trophy on their desk or computer until someone else earns the honor.

One recent semester, I didn't have to work so hard to encourage questions. That's because I had Elina in my class. Elina Kozmits had emigrated from Russia just eighteen months before and was competing with native speakers in an upper division writing course at a Big Ten University. She's obviously a remarkable woman, and what was most remarkable about her was her wonderful willingness to ask questions.

"What is this 'off the wall'?" she asked when I used that phrase. "Who is Elberta McKnight?" she asked after I got done savaging local television news reporting. "I don't understand," she said often. "Please explain."

Golden words, an admission, not of stupidity, but of ignorance, combined with a fierce determination to learn.

I noticed a lot of heads nodding whenever she asked a question. Other students wanted and needed the answers, too. But only Elina asked. No wonder she had come so far and done so well.

Be Absolutely Open About Your Ignorance

As we grow up, we presume to understand our world. Even when we don't understand, we pretend we do. Wouldn't it be better to ask?

"Excuse me, but is that mushroom edible?"

Why take a chance? In fact, with a question like that, you'd better heed the old reporter's axiom: "If your mother says she loves you, get a second source."

A master writer empties herself of pretense and presumption. At the risk of appearing stupid, she asks her question, because she wants and needs to know. Master writer and reporter Cynthia Gorney of the *Washington Post* says she has learned to be absolutely open about her ignorance. The only stupid question, she says, is the one she fails to ask.

Before she interviews a source, she prepares as much as she can. She learns about the source and about the area under discussion, but not so that she can show off her learning. She readies herself so that she can ask good questions and understand the answers. When she doesn't understand, she asks more questions until she does.

"Find someone who speaks 'laymanese,' and just keep asking questions," says Patrick Young, chief science and medical writer for the Newhouse newspaper chain. Young won't even write something down on his notepad, he says, until he can understand it. That way, he won't be tempted to pass on incomprehensible jargon to his reader.

Who's That Rookie Asking All the Dumb Questions?

While attending a writing conference in Iowa City, I bumped into a friend and colleague, Bill Nelson, who writes and edits for *Wisconsin*, the Sunday magazine of the *Milwaukee Journal*. Bill's a seasoned freelancer, with well over 1,000 articles to his credit. He also does a great deal of teaching for the University Outreach where I work. Bill probably knows as much about freelancing as anybody alive.

And yet, at every workshop he attended that day, he was front row center, taking notes and asking questions. You would have thought him the greenest beginner in the room. Bill's always asking questions and always learning. That's why he's so good at what he does.

The only dumb question is the one you didn't ask because you were too shy, or too concerned about maintaining an aura of knowledgeability and intelligence, to ask.

"There's Just One Thing I Don't Understand"

Master reporter/writers like Gorney, Young and Nelson give us wonderful role models for childlike inquisitiveness, but Peter Falk provides an even better model. Falk created the role of Columbo, the rumpled police lieutenant who, notebook in hand, cigar stub in mouth, keeps asking seemingly stupid questions, lulling the murderer into feeling superior and letting down the guard. Criminals underestimate him right up until the moment he springs the trap he has carefully constructed out of the details he has gathered.

Columbo observes the small, seemingly unimportant details and makes his deductions based on this evidence. Writers create articles, stories, poems and novels from such details and call them quotes and anecdotes, dialogue and images.

"If You Could Be Any Twee, What Twee Would You Be?"

Barbara Walters once said that she felt privileged to interview all those famous people on her television specials, because she got to ask questions on behalf of all of us. She always tried to imagine what questions we'd want to ask, she said, if we could be there.

If you could host the Cosmic Talk Show and have as your guest anyone now living or who ever lived, who would you choose and what questions would you ask?

Asking Every Stupid Question You Ever Wanted to Ask

In the last chapter, you brainstormed "how come?" questions. Now let's open up the process to any kind of question. Take a look around you. See anything you don't understand? Anything you'd like to know more about? Anything that doesn't quite add up? Take fifteen to twenty minutes to create a list of questions. Don't hold back, and don't evaluate. Just jot them down. When you've finished, sit still for a few minutes and see if anything else will come.

Then take your notebook with you for a few days and add to your list. Every time you encounter a wonderment, write it down.

Brainstorm your initial list before reading on. Then over the next few days, select a few of your questions and pursue the answers.

Twenty-Five Fabulously Foolish Questions
Here are a few questions I came up with by brainstorming and then by noting other questions as they occurred to me later.

1. What happens to the caps after military cadets toss them at graduation? Do they have to retrieve their own hats? If so, how do they ever find them? Is the hat-throwing a prescribed part of the ceremony, or just something the cadets do? Does anybody get in trouble for it?

2. Who put the "X" in "Xmas"?

3. How does a three-way light bulb work? For that matter, how does a one-way bulb work?

4. When does the speed limit on the traffic sign take effect? Are you supposed to slow down as soon as you can read the sign? If so, do they assume 20/20 vision? Or do you get a grace period after the sign to slow down?

5. What does the "M&M" on those little candies stand for, if anything?

6. Is Chicago really windier than other cities?

7. Which do Americans keep more of, dogs or cats?

8. Can you tell a boy cat from a girl cat just by looking? If so, how?

9. What kind of fish is a sardine?

10. Do fish sleep?

11. Do any other creatures besides humans get a sunburn?

12. What's the difference between a pig and a hog?

13. How does a snake move?

14. Why do we call detectives "private eyes"?

15. Why shouldn't we look a gift horse in the mouth?

16. Did anyone really write "Chopsticks"? Or did it just sort of happen?

17. What does "auld lang syne" mean?

18. Do identical twins have the same fingerprints?

19. Why do we have fingerprints — other than so that the FBI can keep track of us?

20. What does the ZIP in "ZIP Code" stand for?

21. What's the best-selling cookie in America?

22. What does "Kemo Sabe" mean? (In case you've forgotten or never knew, that's what Tonto called the Lone Ranger.)

23. On a clear night, when you're stargazing, how many stars can you gaze at once?

24. Why does Ivory soap float? Did they do it on purpose?

25. How much beef does McDonald's use in a year?

Curiosity killed the cat, so the expression goes. But do you know how that adage ends? Information brought him back to life. So now, with the help of David Feldman and Barbara Berliner, whom you met in the last chapter, along with a few other handy sources, here are:

Twenty-Five Fabulously Fascinating Answers

1. What happens to the caps after the cadets toss them at graduation?
They let kids have them. Although not a scheduled part of the ceremony, cap throwing has become a kind of a spontaneous tradition. Nobody gets in trouble.

2. Who put the "X" in "Xmas"?
Actually, "Xmas" isn't, as you might think, a recent, crass attempt to commercialize Christmas by removing the central character from the celebration. The "X" goes all the way back to a Greek letter first used to stand for "Christ" in about A.D. 1100. So "Xmas" legitimately means "Christ's mass," and "Xianity" is a valid substitute for "Christianity."

3. How does a three-way light bulb work?
When you turn on the light, you complete an electrical circuit, causing electricity to heat a thin wire called a *filament*, which glows,

creating light. It took Edison several hundred tries to find the right filament for the job, by the way.

The first two wattages on a three-way bulb always add up to the amount of the third and highest wattage. How come? A three-way bulb has two filaments, a 50- and a 100-watter, let's say. The low setting heats up the 50. Medium uses the 100. High gets you the 50 plus the 100 for 150.

Now somebody explain to me how those lamps turn on when you touch them and how some lights go on when you clap your hands.

4. When does the speed limit on the sign take effect?
You're supposed to be going the new speed as you pass the sign.

5. What does the "M&M" stand for?
Mars and Murrie (or Merrie, depending on which source you believe), big candy honchos in the 1940s.

You knew, of course, that they dunk the little rascals to get the shell on, and that's why there's no seam.

6. Is Chicago really windier than other cities?
Myth busting time. According to a recent survey, Chicago ranks no better than sixteenth on the list of windiest American cities. The winner? Great Falls, Montana, a tough place to keep your Stetson on your head.

7. Which do Americans keep more of, dogs or cats?
According to 1988 figures, cats have passed dogs as America's favorite house pet. We keep almost 58 million cats but "only" a shade under 49.5 million doggies.

Over 37 percent of American households have at least one dog, while the figure for cats is right around 30 percent, so somebody's keeping a whole lot of cats.

8. Can you tell a boy cat from a girl cat just by looking? If so, how?
According to the experts, you can tell by lifting the cat's tail. If what you see resembles a colon (as in the punctuation mark, not the internal organ), you're dealing with the hind end of a male. If it looks more like an upside-down semi-colon, you've got a female.

But how do you get the cat to hold still for this inspection?

9. What kind of fish is a sardine?
Sardines can be any one of a number of species of herring.

10. Do fish sleep?
With rare exceptions, no.

11. Do any other creatures besides humans get a sunburn?
Only pigs share our propensity for frying the pigment. But I've never seen a pig sunbathe.

12. What's the difference between a pig and a hog?
If it tips the scales at 180 pounds or less, call it a pig. Above 180, you've got yourself a hog.

13. How does a snake move?
Last summer I met Fafner, about nine feet worth of Burmese Python. (They get up to twenty-five feet long and can weigh over a hundred pounds, which is a lot of Python.) Fafner's owner, Paul Haugen, let me hold Fafner, or a part of him anyway. It was actually quite a pleasant experience, as snakes are not at all slimy. But after a bit, Fafner got bored and started to leave.

I don't have any idea how he did it. I felt no undulation, no rippling of muscles, no contractions, nothing. He just seemed to glide along my hands without any apparent effort.

Haugen said he didn't know how Fafner did it either. Does anybody?

14. Why do we call detectives "private eyes"?
Apparently the term came from the Pinkerton logo and their slogan, "We never sleep."

Here's your bonus detective question: Who shoplifts more often, men or women?

Women, by a four- or five-to-one ratio. Any idea how come?

15. Why shouldn't we look a gift horse in the mouth?
If you were swapping for or buying a horse, you'd check the horse's teeth as an indication of its overall condition. (I don't know exactly what you're supposed to be looking for in there? Gingivitis? Periodontal disease?)

So if somebody gave you a horse, and you immediately pried

open the horse's mouth for an inspection, you'd be questioning the value of the gift and thus insulting your friend.

16. Did anyone really write "Chopsticks"?
"Chopsticks" was the creation of a sixteen-year-old girl named Euphemia Allen, who penned the immortal classic in 1877 under the name "Arthur de Lulli." So who gets the royalties now?

17. What does "auld lang syne" mean?
"Old long ago" in Scottish.

18. Do identical twins have identical fingerprints?
No.

19. Why do we have fingerprints?
For traction to help us pick things up.

20. What does the ZIP in "ZIP Code" stand for?
Zoning Improvement Plan.

21. What's the best-selling cookie?
The redoubtable Oreo. We buy about six billion a year. You do eat the filling first, don't you? Thought so.

22. What does "Kemo Sabe" mean?
It's *supposed* to mean "faithful friend." To me it always sounded a lot like "Quien sabe," Spanish for "Who knows?"
    In Apache, the phrase means "white shirt." In Navajo, it translates roughly to "Bring me a shrubbery."

23. On a clear night, when you stargaze, how many stars can you gaze at?
About 2,500, with Carl Sagan's "billyuns and billyuns and billyuns" lurking just out of range.

24. Why does Ivory soap float?
Way back in 1879, a worker left the blender running when he went to lunch, and too much air got mixed in with the soap. The resultant mixture floated. A sharp copywriter coined the phrase "It floats," sales went up, and Ivory has been floating ever since.

25. How much beef does McDonald's use in a year?

You've probably heard some variation of the McDonald's joke:

"Wow! McDonald's sells three billion burgers a year."

"Why, good Lord, man! Do you realize that's nearly seven pounds of hamburger meat?"

Actually, McDonald's does sell about three billion burgers a year, using, not seven, but 560 million pounds of beef.

Some of Our Answers Come From Inside Us

The master writer not only pesters other folks with her queries, but she asks *herself* a lot of stupid questions. She knows that only she has the answers to some of her questions and that she can reach the answers only by asking herself the right stupid questions. The answers can lead to new creation, in the writer and in the writing.

Mike Baron created a successful comic book, *Nexus*, a combination of "Kung Fu," "Have Gun Will Travel" and "Star Trek," only weirder. When *Nexus* became a big seller, Mike's editors wanted him to come up with another idea. They insisted that he base the comic on yet another costumed, crime-fighting superhero, because that's what sells.

Mike struggled with (or against) the notion for a bit. And then he asked himself the right stupid question: "What kind of a person puts on a costume and fights crime?" Then he answered himself: "You'd have to be crazy to do a thing like that." Bingo. Mike created *Badger* — the only comic book superhero with a multiple personality psychosis.

Michael Keaton seems to have embraced Baron's concept. Keaton says that he played *Batman* in the movie basically as a psychologically troubled guy who doesn't get enough sleep.

■ ■ ■ ■ ■ ■ ■ ■ ■ ■ ■ ■ ■ ■ ■ ■ ■ ■ ■

Exploration:
Interviewing Your Muse

 Before Freud came along and took a lot of the fun out of things, we used to picture creative inspiration as a muse whispering precious phrases into our ears. In the movie *Alice*, Woody Allen created a flesh and blood muse, played by Bernadette Peters, for his title character, played by Mia Farrow. Alice actually gets to talk to her muse. Doesn't seem to help, though. Alice still has to rely on strange teas and magic powders to get out of herself and into her creative mode.

What does your muse look like? Would you cast Bernadette Peters in the role? Peter Falk? Bart Simpson? Perhaps your muse looks just like you. Your muse might change appearance from day to day, minute to minute.

Conduct a dialogue on paper between you and your muse. Lose control of the conversation and see where the muse wants to take you. Ask your muse every question you've ever had about your writing. Ask how writing fits into your life. Ask how life fits into your writing. Ask anything. Then let the muse answer.

Tell your muse exactly what kind of inspiration you want. Trust the muse to give you what you need. You have all the answers within you.

Try this exploration more than once. While writing this book, I've had conversations with many muses. Here's how one of those conversations turned out.

The Muse in the Rumpled Trenchcoat

He knocks timidly on my office door and sticks his head in.

"Excuse me?"

I'm at the keyboard, struggling. Words come, but there's nothing behind them. I am, as they say, uninspired. Bad time for an interruption, but then, when's a good time?

"Yeah. What can I do for you?"

"I'm sorry to interrupt, sir. I wonder if I could have a moment of your time."

"Sure. Come on in."

"Thank you. I really appreciate this, sir. I know how busy you are, a successful writer such as yourself. It must be one thing after another."

He's looking past me at the computer screen. I regret not having put the screen on moire idle. I hate it when somebody looks at the meatloaf while it's still in the oven.

The hand he pokes toward the screen holds about two inches of unlit cigar between stubby index and middle fingers.

"Is that a new book you're working on there, sir?"

He is the proverbial unmade bed—disheveled mop of

black hair, rumpled trenchcoat, wrinkled, soiled white shirt, tie askew. Even his eyes seem messy; they don't quite point in the same direction.

"Yes. As a matter of fact, it is."

"Ooh." He bends to look at the screen and nearly tips over my coffee mug. "Isn't that something?" he says.

"Are you a writer?"

"Me? Oh, no, sir." He straightens up, hands in front of his face as if fending off the suggestion. "My wife, *she's* the writer in the family. She's terrific. I write a little bit. As a matter of fact, I started a novel once."

"Oh, really." Here it comes. He's got a six-trillion page manuscript, written in Crayola on butcher paper. It's the story of his life, or the story of his immigrant grandparents, or a humorous look at toilet fixtures throughout the ages. Would I mind taking a look at it?

"May I?"

I motion him into one of the chairs around my little conference table. He collapses into the chair in a way that suggests he doesn't plan to get up again for a long time, perhaps never.

"I don't suppose I'd better . . . " He gestures vaguely with the cigar.

"University rules," I say, sounding as if, were it left to me, I'd like nothing better than to have him fire up his portable smudge pot.

He smiles, nods. I wait for a question. When none comes, I say, "So tell me about this novel of yours."

He growls, waving it away. "It's just something I play around with in my spare time. It deals with my experiences on the force."

"The force?"

"Yes, sir. I'm a police officer. Thirty years next January."

"Really?" I'm genuinely surprised. I would have taken him for a mattress salesman. "How interesting."

"Oh, yes, sir. It is. I could tell you stories. Well, that's what the novel's all about, of course. I guess you'd call it more of an autobiography, except that I've changed things around some. Taken some liberties." He smiles. I see now that he has a decided cast in one eye. It's probably glass, although I'm not sure. The western sky has clouded up outside my window, and my visitor is sitting in shadow.

"To protect the innocent."

"Well . . . " He chuckles. "More to make the stories work out better," he says. He looks down at his cigar.

"We must lie to achieve a higher truth," I say, "a feeling-level truth."

He looks up, eyes wide. "That's very good, sir," he says, fumbling a notebook and pencil from an inside coat pocket. "Do you mind if I write that down?"

"Of course not. But it's hardly original with me."

"Very well put, though, sir. Very well put."

His lips move as he writes Ben Logan's aphorism in his little notebook. The pencil is little more than a stub. I think I see teeth marks. I wait for him to finish. He squints up at me.

"So it's okay, then? To change things around like that?"

"Okay with whom? We do whatever the writing needs."

"Oh, yes, sir. Very good, sir."

He scribbles another note, filling the little page with his thick scrawl. "Whatever it takes," he mumbles. Then he says, "Is that the sort of thing you're putting in your new book, sir?"

The question catches me off stride. I had expected the standard, "How do I get an agent?"

"I'm trying not to be too preachy. Let the reader discover her own truth."

He nods, hunches forward, and suddenly we're a part of some conspiracy. He reaches out with the chubby, cigar-bearing hand and gently touches my arm. "That's very profound, sir," he says, his gravelly voice dropping to little more than a whisper.

"Hardly profound."

He makes a shushing noise, waving the cigar in my face. I catch a stale whiff. "You'd be surprised the kind of impact you have, sir. My wife read your first book through twice. Every word. She read me passages in bed. Oh, yes, sir." He chuckles. "You've wakened me out of a sound sleep many times."

"If I've helped, even a little . . . "

"Oh, you've helped a great deal, sir. You have no idea."

"That's very nice to hear."

The little gnome is beaming at me. Both eyes seem to twinkle.

"Well," he says, putting his palms flat on the table and shoving to his feet. "I've taken up enough of your time."

"Not at all." I rise with him.

For a moment I think I'm going to have to shake the cigar, but he transfers it to his other hand before extending his pudgy paw over the table.

"My wife will be thrilled when I tell her I talked with you," he says.

"Have her give me a call. We'll talk writing."

"Really? Oh, sir. You don't mean it. Give you a call, just like that?"

"Absolutely."

"Well," he says, shaking his head. "It just shows to go you. The bigger they are, the nicer they are."

"It would be my pleasure. And come again. I want to hear how that book of yours comes out."

"Isn't that something," he says, backing out the door.

I turn back to my screen, put my fingers to the keyboard.

"Oh, sir?"

He has reappeared in the doorway.

"I'm sorry, sir. Just one more question, if I may?"

"Certainly."

"What would you call it, sir? The kind of book that's based on fact but changes things around to make the stories work out better."

I think about that. "I don't think it matters what you call it," I say. "I guess I'd call it 'The Great Book of Your Life.' "

"Ah, sir," he says, chuckling and pointing at me with the cigar. "That's very good, sir. Thank you, sir."

I watch the door this time to be sure he has really gone. Something on the table snags a corner of my eye. He has left his grubby little notebook. I jump up, run out into the hall, but the hall is empty. Strange. I had heard neither the click of the door to the stairs nor the thump of the elevator doors closing.

I can't resist looking at the page he has covered with scrawls.

"Do whatever it takes to make it work."

I return to the screen and to my stalled work. As I reread the last words I've written, the next ones begin to form. I write steadily and well until my back aches and my stomach growls with hunger.

7

Seeing With Eyes of Wonder

Be quite still and solitary. The world will freely offer
itself to you to be unmasked. It has no choice.
It will roll in ecstasy at your feet.
— *Franz Kafka*

When you were a kid, everything was new to you, and so you looked intently at every tree, frog and dog. Each encounter was a new mystery. You probably stared at people a lot. Your stare could be quite intimidating, I imagine, but you didn't mean to be impolite. You hadn't learned about polite yet. You just wanted to look.

Too soon we learn to look away. Just try catching someone's eye the next time you walk down the street. As we mature, we learn to see only what we want, need or expect to see. We learn to chunk things into categories labeled "tree," "frog," "dog," "woman" and the like, and then we don't need to look so intently at each specific manifestation of the general. We only need to identify it and put it in the proper mental bin.

Just as we assume to know all the answers to those "stupid questions," once we get something or someone placed in the proper category, we assume we know all about it, too.

Sometimes this tendency can confuse us. Perhaps you've had this experience. You're walking down a deserted city street early in the morning. You see a figure approaching, still several blocks away. You can't yet make out the particulars, but there's something familiar about this figure, something about the silhouette or the way of walking. Based on these clues, you think you know this person, and you prepare your greeting.

But as the figure draws nearer, something seems wrong, and you begin to make a mental adjustment. Other details aren't supporting your original conclusion, but your mind seems reluctant to abandon it. When the figure is but a block away, you realize that it isn't the person you thought it was at all. In fact, as you cross paths, you realize that the stranger doesn't look anything like your friend. How could you have been so mistaken?

Your conscious, controlling mind can't stand ambiguity and won't tolerate random, meaningless information from the environment. So you try to make sense out of whatever you encounter. We all do it. When we look up at the stars, for example, instead of seeing random dots and washes of light, we imagine that we see hunters and crabs and other patterns.

We make complex assumptions about people based on sparse, gene al clues. For example, suppose that person walking down the deserted city street toward you has long, unwashed hair and a beard stubble. Suppose that his clothes are little better than rags, that he walks with a limp and that he carries a plastic garbage bag filled with who-knows-what slung over his shoulder.

Based on that information, some of us would put the man into a category marked "bum, street person, drug addict." Some might cross the street to avoid passing close to such a person. For others, the label might read "poor unfortunate," and they might begin searching their pockets for spare change.

But human beings have a wonderful capacity to surprise, to climb out of the bins we try to put them into. As you pass, this "street person" may look up, flash you a glorious "good morning" smile, and wink. Where is the depravity? Where is the raw need? We need a new category for this one.

My friend Paul Ashe runs a meals program out of a church basement on the campus where I teach. A different church group volunteers to provide, prepare and serve the food each noon. Ashe insists that they also sit down and eat with those they are serving.

"We're really not so different," Ashe says. "We have a lot to learn from each other."

Ashe refuses to label the people he helps to feed. He encounters them as individuals. He loves many of them. Some he could get along just fine without. But he insists that everyone who comes to that church basement treat everyone else with dignity and respect. He says he feels privileged to share food and company with them, and he means it.

Mostly, we learn to screen out the street people and other unpleasant elements in our environment. And we screen out the merely irrelevant, too, not just the street beggar but the street musician, who offers wonderful diversion if we'll but stop the mad march and stand still for a moment.

We lose much of the life around us because we never see it. We already "know" about stars, so we stop looking at the stars at all. When was the last time you walked outside at night and stared up at the sky, simply letting the wonderment wash over you?

"The world will never starve for want of wonders," G.K. Chesterton wrote, "but only for want of wonder."

A Walk With an Arborist

One cool, northern Wisconsin summer morning, I had the joy of taking a walk with Bruce Allison, nature writer and tree doctor.

Bruce loves trees. As with any true love, Bruce delights in learning ever more about the objects of his affection. As a consequence, he sees things I've never noticed.

For instance, that lump on the trunk of a slender poplar? (I had thought it was a birch, but Bruce set me straight.) That's a gall. It's formed when a parasite burrows into the host tree and actually alters the genetic structure of the messenger RNA, so that, instead of growing straight or producing a limb or whatever the tree was supposed to do, it grows a pouch or gall instead, giving the parasite nourishment and a cozy home. I not only didn't know what a gall was, but I had never even seen one. Now I see them all the time.

Bruce next pointed out a ring of cones about halfway up a pine tree. I hadn't noticed the cones or the fact that no cones grew below that halfway point. They're up that high so that animals can't nibble on them, Bruce explained, and also so that the seeds will blow far enough away to take root away from the shade of the mama tree.

Bruce wasn't showing off his knowledge. His lessons were imparted unself-consciously. Because he loves the trees, he wants to know everything about them, and he assumes that his listeners do, too.

I thought I knew trees, but I didn't know trees. Now I'm learning about trees, looking at them more carefully, noticing the differences. Now when I pass a fresh tree stump, I mourn the death of the tree and wonder if the death was necessary. To know is to love. To love is to pay attention.

If we don't pay attention, we create descriptions based on our false sense of knowing, based on generalizations and on descriptions we've read before, and not on the specific reality we really need to describe. Instead of creating a vision for the reader, we talk about the vision, and the reader only hears us talking and sees nothing.

"Don't write about Man," E.B. White advised. "Write about *a* man." But you can only do that when you've really *seen* that man.

Unleashing the Adjectives

I'm often amazed by the descriptions my students write. Some of the writers who have been struggling to master news or feature article structure or who have been having a hard time learning to develop and pursue sources present me with stunningly careful and evocative description. But too often the converse is true. Students who write clean, crisp articles plunge into a strange twilight zone of cliché, pretentious prose and borrowed detail. They've apparently been saving up all those adjectives I wouldn't let them use in a news story, and they allow them to swarm all over their descriptions like angry sweat bees. I don't recognize these artificial voices, and I don't want to spend much time listening to them.

Here's a bit of description from an otherwise fine writer and reporter who graced my writing lab one recent semester:

> My eyes, adjusting to the ebony surroundings, begin to play with . . . the stars which shine so faintly from above . . . . The lonely trees stand tall among the remaining snowdrifts that crowd around their trunks. The stars have quieted and seem singular in their brilliance. The moonlight has succumbed its weary head to the amber ray that lurks on the horizon.

Strong verbs like "lurks" help her to create a mood here, but I can't see those "singular" stars, "lonely" trees or "amber" ray. This writing doesn't put me into the scene. It simply tells me how the writer feels about it. And who is this strange creature, who uses words like "ebony"? I never heard her talk that way. I wonder why she felt the need to assume such a voice in her descriptive writing.

The master writer recultivates the ability to look intensely and carefully, with eyes of childlike wonder, at the commonplace world around her. She sees the specific, as it really is, and not as she imagines or supposes it to be. Only then will she write with certainty and originality about her world. Her descriptions draw on her observations and not on the stale words of others. She writes with clarity and precision, without adopting pretentious voices or poses. Her writing conveys mood and theme because she chooses her details carefully. Her descriptions are purposeful.

He Had Gone Eighty-Four Days Now Without Taking a Fish

Read again, carefully, the way Hemingway describes his old fisherman, Santiago, at the beginning of *The Old Man and the Sea*:

> The old man was thin and gaunt with deep wrinkles in the back of his neck. The brown blotches of the benevolent skin cancer the sun brings from its reflection on the tropic were on his cheeks. The blotches ran well down the sides of his face and his hands had the deep-creased scars from handling heavy fish on the cords. But none of these scars were fresh. They were as old as erosions in a fishless desert. Everything about him was old except his eyes and they were the same color as the sea and were cheerful and undefeated.

Hemingway will ask us to accept this old fisherman as a representative of humanity, but he is an individual human being, and Hemingway lets us see him (and see into him, too, to the soul that cannot be defeated).

In the same way, Ken Kesey wants us to see a particular river at the beginning of his masterpiece, *Sometimes a Great Notion*, and to understand the river's symbolic significance to the Stamper family.

> . . . a vast smile of water with broken and rotting pilings jagged along both gums, foam clinging to the lips. Closer still, it flattens into a river, flat as a street . . . flat as a rain-textured street even during flood season because of a channel so deep and a bed so smooth . . . A river smooth and seeming calm, hiding the cruel file-edge of its current beneath a smooth and calm-seeming surface.

Do you have any doubt that this river will play a large role in the survival drama to follow?

Here's another master writer, Aldo Leopold, describing a scene and drawing conclusions in his masterwork, *A Sand County Almanac*.

> The skunk track enters the woods, and crosses a glade where the rabbits have packed down the snow with their tracks, and mottled it with pinkish urinations. Newly exposed oak seed-

lings have paid for the thaw with their newly barked stems. Tufts of rabbit-hair bespeak the year's first battles among the amorous bucks. Further on I find a bloody spot, encircled by a wide-sweeping arc of owl's wings. To this rabbit the thaw brought freedom from want, but also a reckless abandonment of fear. The owl has reminded him that thoughts of spring are no substitute for caution.

To describe with this kind of precision, grace and purpose, Leopold must first see.

Here's master writer Natalie Goldberg, in her wonderful *Writing Down the Bones*, describing a specific encounter with a class full of students and also describing that tendency in us all to generalize:

I walk into the classroom in Elkton, Minnesota. Early April the fields around the school are wet, unplowed, not seeded yet. And the sky is deep gray. I tell the twenty-five eighth graders that I am a Jew after I hear that rabbis is one of their spelling words. None of them has ever seen a Jew before. I am aware that everything I do now for the next hour represents "Jew." I walk in eating an apple: all Jews now will eat apples. I tell them I have never lived in a small town: now no Jew has ever lived in the country.

She goes on to describe the children.

They are very warm and there's a beautiful depth of vulnerability about them. They know what well the water they drink comes from, that their cat who ran away two years ago will not return, how their hair feels against their heads as they run. I don't have to give them any rules about poetry. They live in that place already. Close to things.

The master writer, like the child, lives close to things. And so, when she writes of these things, they are specific and real.

Put a Pretend Camera Around Your Neck

My photographer friend Shiela Reaves says that having a camera around your neck gives you access to living on a more intense level. "You see more intently," she says. So why couldn't a writer hang a pretend camera around her neck and go out looking for pictures?

The most important piece of equipment for the photographer

isn't the fancy camera, the "techno stuff," Shiela insists. It's the head and the heart of the photographer.

"Listen to your instincts," she says. "Your natural curiosity is so important."

For the writer, too.

Change your point of view, Shiela says. Get up high and look down on Mother Earth. Or get down low and emphasize the sky. If it works for a photographer, why shouldn't it work for a writer? Stand on the tabletop. Get down on the floor. See your world from a different angle.

The photographer sees the pattern of the tire tracks in the snow, Shiela says, then waits for ten or fifteen minutes for a pedestrian to break the pattern. The writer can look for those patterns and for ways to break the patterns, too.

The photographer plays with light and shadow, Shiela says. She looks for the side lighting from the window to provide shadows and highlights on her subject's face. She looks for backlighting to cast her subject in silhouette and create an aura of light around it. The writer can look for light and shadow, too.

"Pay attention to the here and now, the simple here and now," Shiela says. "We can never go back." So true for the photographer. So true for the writer.

■ ■ ■ ■ ■ ■ ■ ■ ■ ■ ■ ■ ■ ■ ■ ■

Exploration: Writing From the Inside Out

 Take an object with which you're thoroughly familiar: your vacuum cleaner, a daisy, an English muffin. First write a description of it, based on your prior knowledge of the object and other objects like it. Set this description aside.

Spend five minutes examining the object carefully. See how it's different from any other vacuum cleaner, daisy, or English muffin in the world. Write a second description, focusing on those differences. This way, you can't write about "daisy" in general; you have to write about this particular daisy.

You may create some of the most powerful writing you've ever done.

Compare your descriptions. How is the second different from the first? Is it in any sense better than the first? Compare your descriptions to the object itself. Have you captured the essence? What, if anything, is missing from your description? What have you added?

Don't worry about whether or not your writing is "important" or "significant." Let your reader decide what the daisy "means" or "represents." For you, it must be enough to get the daisy right, to let it be its own reason for being.

Write your descriptions before reading my general description of an object I know well.

Ode on an Oat Scone

The scone is round and mounded, like a large grainy hockey puck, maybe four inches across and not quite an inch high. It's the color of a dusty road, and crumbly like a dirt clod with just a little moisture left in it. The surface is bumpy and cratered. It's heavier than it looks like it should be.

Folks cannot live by scone alone.

It's a comfort, having that scone in my backpack for later. You won't ever go hungry with a scone in your backpack.

Not much of a smell to it, not like having carried a sack of red onions around with you for a morning.

Not so much a taste as a texture, a comfort for mouth and soul, a heartiness. It's solid. A gentle sweetness, the surprise of an occasional date or raisin, and mostly the solid bread essence. A thing of substance is the oat scone. Yield of the good earth and work of human hands. A scone isn't just made. It's prepared.

Now here's my description of a specific oat scone.

My Friday, May 3, 1991, Steep & Brew Oat Scone

Slightly browned, with white blotches of unmixed flour. A dent, like a cove or shoreline cave. A few unmixed oats, and a few raisins showing. Cracks and a gully, like erosion in an arroyo. A little bit of a sheen to it, like maybe the baker coated it with butter before baking.

Even the parts that look smooth feel rough. A light powder covers the scone. For something so solid, it seems rather fragile. If I dropped it, it might burst into fragments and would at least chip.

Close up, I get that nice baked bread smell, but I have to work at it. I'll bet an oven full of these fills a room with joy.

This scone is mute, but I don't think it's dumb. I think it's just waiting, keeping its own council. This is a wise and patient scone. Life is hard; the scone accepts that. Loud good times don't offer long-lasting satisfaction, the scone tells me.

The young lady at the next table has her scone upside down on its cellophane paper — signal for distress? Like a turtle, it cannot right itself.

Another young lady at a nearby table has a lemon poppy seed muffin. Now there's a fleeting, airy thing. Not like this solid scone. My scone says permanence. Eat me, and I will be with you always.

Can I really put this friend scone back in the bag and not eat it until noon? It will be good to travel with a scone for a time before eating him.

I think yes.

See First, Then Write What You See

By cultivating the habit of first seeing clearly and then rendering a clear, specific description of what you've seen, you will teach yourself to write with accuracy, originality and power. You will combine the child's ability to see with the master's ability to express. In turn, your reader will see and experience the reality you create.

8

Writing Spontaneously and Holding Nothing Back

> By now this old typewriter knows where to go on its own,
> and I just follow along.
> —*Robert Siegel*

Children often act first and think later—if at all. They are innocent of consequences.

Jeremiah once smashed our kitchen window with a hammer, not because he wished the window any harm, but simply, he told us later, because he didn't know what would happen and wanted to find out.

He learned that windows break if you hit them with hammers. Ellen and I learned about glazier's points and window putty.

Innocence dies in the learning. Jeremiah couldn't smash another window with a hammer and plead ignorance as a defense.

Children are spontaneous. They hold nothing back. They'll tell you exactly what they think. Art Linkletter made a career out of this trait of children, first by interviewing kids every day on his "House Party" program, and later by collecting their wit and wisdom in a book called *Kids Say the Darndest Things* ("darndest" apparently translating to "utterly embarrassing to their parents").

Kids just let it rip. They do no more intellectualizing about what they're doing than does a chicken when it lays an egg.

Your *Savoir Faire* Needs Clipping

Some writers are able to re-create the illusion of this childish lack of inhibition in their writing. Read a collection of essays by Dave Barry, and you'll see what I mean. Dave seems to write whatever pops into his head, kayaking on his stream-of-consciousness, careening from one outrageous exaggeration to the next out-and-out falsehood, all the while snickering and capering and seeming to have a wonderful time.

Here's a sample from a recent Dave Barry column, in which he "apologizes" (fat chance) for a "factual error" made in a previous column:

> ... I was incorrect when I stated that *savoir faire* is French for "ear size," as in the sentence "Prince Charles and President Bush are men of great *savoir faire*." ... Needless to say, I feel like a total Mr. Potato Head (or, as the French say, "un total Monsieur Tete de la Pomme de Terre") about this. I deeply regret the error, and I wish to make this formal correction: *Savoir faire* does NOT mean "ear size." It means "nose hair," as in the expression: "Garçon! What are those *savoir faires* doing in my soup?"

Dave says he prides himself on having absolutely nothing in his column that is factually correct. "I want it to read as if I'd written it in ten minutes, while I was drunk," he says. But the fact is, he works extremely hard to achieve this sense of ease and spontaneity, often spending hours at the computer with only a usable sentence or two to show for it.

For kids it comes naturally. Adults have to work at it.

It Has Been a Quiet Week . . .

Novelist T.R. Pearson (*A Brief History of a Small Place, The Last of How It Was* and others) provides another fine example of a seemingly spontaneous style. His nearly endless sentences and paragraphs take us on plot digression after plot digression as we meander through Pearson's rural South.

Garrison Keillor's Lake Wobegon monologues on the popular Minnesota Public Radio program "A Prairie Home Companion" have the same sense of spontaneity and digression. Keillor conducts his forty-minute tours without a note or a cue card, with eyes closed, cradling the microphone in his large hands, swaying almost imperceptibly to the rhythms of his language.

And yet, for all the surprises, for all the wonderful scenery, Pearson and Keillor always drop us off exactly where they picked us up, every loose end bound, every reference developed. There is much craft behind their seeming lack of intention. It's a true merger of spontaneous child and master storyteller.

Teach Your Children Well

We love and envy and sometimes even resent kids for their freedom. Oh, to be so uninhibited. Some folks delight in a child's behavior. Others are made nervous, even frantic by it (and may take to issuing nonsensical commands such as "Act your age," which is, of course, precisely what the child is doing). But no matter how we feel, we know we must teach our children to be cautious, to look both ways, if they are to survive. Sometimes the results of childish experimentation can be a lot more disastrous than a broken window. A child may dart out into traffic, may fling herself wildly from the swing onto the concrete, may blurt out a conversation-stopping comment at the dinner table.

Children become teenagers. It's an unhappy fact of nature. "Bigger kids mean bigger trouble," the adage warns. But if teenagers become no more cautious in their behaviors, they do rein in their individuality in some important ways. The first pimple appears, and the former free spirit becomes paralyzed with self-consciousness. A kid whose total notion of hygiene once involved rubbing filthy hands on a towel before dinner, and then only in response to parental prodding, suddenly spends hours in the shower. A child who took no notice of what anyone else wore now has to achieve the proper "look," as defined by the peer group.

Back when I was a teener, the "look" meant a swept-back hairdo called a "D.A." (the "D" stood for "duck's," and that's as much as you'll get out of me), black (not blue—sorry Elvis) suede shoes guaranteed to become ruined within seven minutes of first being worn, the inevitable Levi's (just Levi's—I predate the age of the stone-washed, pretorn jeans and that ultimate status symbol, jeans that have been shot up by a Tennessee mountain man or worn by a Montana cowboy), and a white T-shirt with sleeves rolled precisely twice, never once, never thrice, but twice (preferably to hold a pack of cigarettes and certainly, in my case, not to reveal bulging biceps).

We followed rather rigid guidelines in achieving our nonconformity. We all had to look and sound like James Dean and dance to Jan and Dean.

The "look" now seems to involve a little tail of hair snaking down the neck, T-shirts with satanic messages on them, jeans that look as if they've been put through a paper shredder, and two or three rings in each nostril. Just as in the "old days," the totally outrageous, nonconformist style has all the originality and spontaneity of an army uniform, but whatever the style, it drives parents bananas (which is, of course, a major part of the point).

We may remain paralyzed in our need for acceptance based on conformity long after our complexions have cleared up and the senior prom is just a memory. "What will people think?" may remain a more important question than, "What do *I* think?"

Tennessee Williams gave us a painful example of this sort of self-consciousness with Laura Wingfield in *The Glass Menagerie*. Laura had a childhood bout with pleurisy (or "pleurosis," and thus her high school nickname, "Blue Roses") and walks with a limp. But when she tells an old high school classmate of the acute embarrassment her "deformity" caused her—causes her still—he responds with surprise, maintaining that others weren't even aware of the limp.

Laura has allowed herself to be emotionally and spiritually crippled. All that pain, all that waste—and others weren't even looking.

The Class of '62 Had Its Dreams

When I attended my high school reunion, I had a chance to chat with a legend. Rod Sherman had dominated our huge class. (The Class of '62, John Muir High School, Pasadena, California, numbered 1,001.) He was student body president and star varsity quarterback, shortstop and hurdler. He dated the class queen, got top marks and was a wonderful guy to boot. (Who says "It all evens out"?)

When Rod started talking about how self-conscious he was in high school and how painful it had all been at times, I realized that the pain and the self-consciousness are universal to adolescence. We feel it in our own ways, but we all feel it. And we all feel alone in our suffering.

Like the centipede who is asked in what order he moves his legs, we become so self-conscious, we can hardly move at all. We reckon consequences. We take only "calculated risks"—surely as much an oxymoron as "jumbo shrimp" or "genuine plastic."

Such caution, born of self-consciousness and a desire to fit in, can cripple our writing. Our words become a cramped, cautious imitation of the words of others. We edit as we write, not for grammar or clarity alone, but for acceptability and correctness of ideas, approach, attitude. Then we begin to edit *before* we write — and wind up unable to write at all.

Thinking "Wild Thoughts"

The master holds nothing back in her writing.

"A word in that instant of realizing catches fire," writes the poet Alastair Reid, "ignites another, and soon, the page is ablaze with a wildfire of writing." That wildfire may surprise or shock. The master risks all, even risks discovering and revealing herself, which can be the most terrifying prospect of all.

"I have to allow myself to think wild thoughts," says novelist Ben Logan (*The Land Remembers, The Empty Meadow*). "Do I know what it's all about when I write? Usually no.... I simply write, without asking myself what the hell I'm doing."

Interviewer Larry King (not the writer, Larry L. King, but the radio and television personality) refuses to prepare for his interviews with famous writers, performers and politicians. He doesn't create a list of questions, he doesn't read the author's book, he doesn't scan Congressional transcripts. He simply brings his wit, his curiosity and a genuine sense of excitement and spontaneity to each encounter, trying to ask the sort of questions his listeners would ask. Does King know how the interview will turn out? Certainly not. But in allowing for the possibility that he will be just as surprised as his listeners, he gives each interview room to grow and develop.

"All Ways Are My Ways," Says the Queen

When Charles Lutwidge Dodgson undertook to tell a tale about the fantasy explorations of a little girl named Alice, he did so without knowing what she would encounter or how she would react. "I had sent my heroine straight down a rabbit-hole," Dodgson wrote, "without the least idea what was to happen afterwards." Dodgson discovered right along with Alice.

He created a fearless heroine. Alice dared to eat the cake marked "Eat me." She dared to stand up to a tyrant queen who insisted, "All ways are my ways." She dared to try to understand her language even in the face of the assertion that "a word means anything I want it to mean."

Dodgson wasn't as fearless as his creation. He wrote under the pseudonym Lewis Carroll and refused to let the Wonderland part of his personality intrude on his life as Oxford don and mathematician. Perhaps he was ashamed or even frightened of the spontaneous child he had created from the spontaneous child within himself. No matter. We have his Alice to cherish and delight in forever. The creation has become independent of the creator.

The master writer has lost the sweet ignorance of Alice. She creates out of mature awareness of the world, and she knows that the act of writing will have consequences, often painful ones. An action only expresses courage, after all, when the actor is aware of the danger.

She is not innocent of grammar, form and structure, either. She knows what has gone before, and she knows the rules of composition. But she writes as if she were the first writer in the universe, her words the only words that have ever mattered. She will break a rule to create an effect, and she will know she is breaking the rule.

In that way, she combines a child's audacity with an adult's awareness. She leaves it for others to analyze and judge the results.

"When you have done your best, it doesn't matter how good it is," wrote poet and fiction writer Richard Hugo. "That is for others to say."

Breaking Through to Higher Levels

I've been working with an extraordinary student named Dave Fox for almost two years now. Our relationship began when Dave took my newswriting and reporting lab. He told me about a book he wanted to write, based on the journal he kept while traveling through Europe. He became my independent study student so we could work on the project together. He fed me chapters of his work in progress, and I responded, often urging him to loosen up and to supply more detail. At times he seemed to me to be holding back. I urged him to let it rip. I didn't know what the "it" was I wanted him to let rip, but I figured I'd know it if and when I saw it.

Long after our independent study project ended, Dave continued to let me read his work, and we enjoyed frequent conversations about writing and writers, about the contrary ways of book publishers and the ever-elusive Meaning of Life.

After a gap of several weeks, I found a tall stack of computer printout pages in my mailbox and settled down for four more chapters in Dave's saga. I began turning pages with rising excitement, scribbling comments like "Yes!" and "Wow!" in the margins. Dave's writing had always been good—insightful, caustic, wholly original. But this new stuff was intense, full of more emotion, more honest self-revelation, than anything previous. I've never before been privileged to witness such a sudden leap. A good writer had broken through to a higher level.

In part, he had simply written his way into greater awareness of himself and his material. Writing can be as much a matter of discovery for the writer as for the reader. But something else was going on here, and I had to know what.

When Dave came to my office to chat, I of course, shared my reactions and asked if anything in his life accounted for the change I saw in his work. He said that for the past six months he had been grappling with his somewhat stormy childhood, dealing with emotions and issues he thought he had dismissed but had in fact simply buried. We concluded that, although he wasn't writing about any of these things in his book, the openness was pouring over into his travel reflections.

Dave had been holding back from himself—as all of us do—in one area of his life. To withhold in one area is to withhold in all. When he began to let loose and deal with issues of childhood, he began, too, to let loose on the issues of identity and disintegration he dealt with while traveling among strangers in foreign lands.

He had been just about ready to quit a project he had poured himself into for almost two years. But now he is full of big ideas and renewed enthusiasm.

Dave is off to the University in Oslo to study for a year, and he'll be taking the draft of his travel book with him. He'll let it ferment for a bit and then begin the daunting and exciting challenge of re-creating. When he's finished, I think he'll have a book worth reading.

■ ■ ■ ■ ■ ■ ■ ■ ■ ■ ■ ■ ■ ■ ■ ■ ■ ■ ■ ■
Exploration: Seeing Your Own Private Movie

 Why not try a little travel writing of your own? I'll begin a story for you. I want you to read slowly, allowing yourself to picture the scene. Don't worry about getting it "right." Simply see it your way. When I leave off, I want you to put this book down, close your eyes and see what comes next. Don't try to imagine it. Don't force it in any way. Just let the movie that has been running in your mind continue for another minute or so. Go where it takes you.

Then open your eyes, take notebook and pen or pencil, and write down what you saw, just as you saw it. Don't try to shape or organize. Don't search for meaning or significance. Simply write what you saw.

A Walk by the Lake

The August air is heavy with humidity, and the stiff breeze off the lake offers little relief from the heat.

You've been sitting at a table at an outdoor lakeside cafe, sipping your lemonade and nibbling at your fruit cup. Despite the heat, you crave movement. You determine to take a short walk along the lake. You'll be back in plenty of time to keep your appointments.

You set off at a brisk pace, down to the shore and out along the stone retaining wall past the boathouse. The beggar ducks bob along the wall, waiting for you to toss them bread or popcorn, as you have seen others do.

A hundred yards from shore, windsurfers are pounding across the light chop created by the wind. Beyond them, sailboats glide with deceptive serenity.

You walk with the lake to your right. Tall oak trees line the lake path on the left, offering shade. Dense brush fills in the space between the oaks. The breeze rills the leaves of the oaks.

Sweat prickles your forehead and armpits. The walking feels good. You slow your pace, concession to the heat. The path rises, soon offering a steep embankment down to the lake to your right.

You see a break in the brush to your left, a narrow path of stones leading up a gentle slope. On impulse you turn off the main trail and begin to mount the path. Quickly your breath becomes labored, and your sweat runs freely. Ahead, you see a low wall of large, irregular stones. You leave the trail, approach the wall and look over.

Close your eyes. Let yourself see what comes next. Then write it. Don't continue reading until you're finished.

I've had students see many strange and wonderful sights over that wall. A high percentage of young men of a certain age discover a nudist colony. A student occasionally scales the wall and falls into a pit, much like Alice tumbling into Wonderland. Only rarely does a student refuse to look over the wall. It doesn't much matter what you saw; the important thing is *that* you saw—and recorded the image faithfully.

■ ■

Exploration: The Best of Times, The Worst of Times

 Start anywhere and write, without concern for where you'll end up or how you'll get there. You'll write your way into something wonderful and wonderfully revealing.

"We can't not think, not get ideas," the poet William Stafford writes. "Something always occurs."

Or, as writer David Huddle puts it, "One thing leads to another."

For the next couple of weeks, get into the habit of jotting down good first lines as you encounter them. Some will come from your imagination. You'll find others in the newspaper, in a short story, on the lips of a friend, in the conversation at the next table.

After you've developed a list of about twenty first sentences, pick one, write it at the top of the page in your notebook, and simply keep writing for fifteen to twenty minutes. Don't force or direct your writing. Just let the description or narration, the whatever it is or whatever it isn't, go where it needs to. You may get some good, usable stuff. You may not. It doesn't matter. You do this to do it, not to use it.

Here are a few first sentences to get you started. If you find anything here that looks like fun, grab it and go with it.

- "If I had known who she was, do you think I would have talked to her that way?"
- "If we don't stop soon, I believe I shall expire."
- We're so lost, God couldn't find us with a pack of bloodhounds.
- She was the last person on earth I wanted to see.
- Opportunity slipped through my mail slot and plopped

onto my floor—and it sure wasn't the Publisher's Clearinghouse Sweepstakes.

- "Did it ever occur to you that I might not appreciate that kind of remark?"
- He'd give about anything he owned to have the last ten seconds back.
- Still waters run stupid.
- Amanda Louise Sackowitz, three weeks out of business school and still oily behind the ears, approached the receptionist with some considerable trepidation.
- The Reverend Jed liked to tell the story of how he encountered Christ in a Burger King.
- Neil Hartung was ready to sell his soul, but he couldn't find any takers.
- In the split second it took Thelma Jamison to realize that her car keys weren't in her purse where she always kept them, she received a clear and undeniable mental image of the keys dangling from the ignition where she had left them when she locked the car fifteen minutes ago.
- Nolan could account for the headache, the black eye, and the deep red bruise on his abdomen. But he was at a loss to explain his nudity.

Lying and Truth-Telling

A kid will lie. That's part of children's marvelous spontaneity, their lack of care for consequences. They lie to save face and to gain status. They tell stories in which their parents are richer, their houses bigger, their dogs shaggier than anybody else's parents, houses or dogs. The ongoing autobiography of a child is a rich, inventive tapestry of lies.

Some of this comes naturally and is a matter of instinct. But the kids learn a lot about lying from their parents, too. After all, they hear our lies about George Washington and the cherry tree and about Santa Claus and those flying reindeer. We call those "good lies," but they're still lies.

When my best friend Clark Horton moved to Massachusetts from Southern California when we were both about four years old, my mother told me Massachusetts was "just over those mountains." Do you blame her for lying in the face of all my tears? She was only trying to buy me a little time until the pain began to ease and I became old enough to understand.

We teach our kids about "white lies," too. "I don't want to go to your sister's for dinner," they hear us say. "Tell her we're busy that night." And "I think I'll call in sick tomorrow and play some golf." And, "Sure this lunch is deductible. We mentioned the business, didn't we?"

Only a person who likes to inflict—and receive—intense pain would respond with total candor to the question, "Dear, do you think I look fat?"

We not only show kids about lying. Sometimes we even force them into a lie.

"Did you break that vase?" we ask. And the kid hears, "The vase that has been in the family for hundreds of years? The vase that cost a bazillion dollars? The vase for which I will strip the skin off of your hide?"

"Nope. Not me."

Sure, they lie. Can you blame them? Few critters will act contrary to their own self-preservation for the sake of an abstract principle.

As you grew older, you learned that honesty in your dealings with other people is indeed the best policy, not only the nice way to behave but also the smartest. You learned to suppress the urge to lie, and rightly so, as the lie you would tell might be cowardly and hurtful.

But as you become the master writer that is within you, you must draw on your lying child—not to tell the lies that seek to impress with a false image, but the lies that delve deeper than literal truth. Here are some examples of the kind of lies we tell to get out this deeper truth.

Dreams, Memories and Other Lies

Dreams aren't literal or historical truth, so in one sense, they're lies, too. They're actually a creative recombining of stored experience and sense impression. But they often reveal a truth deeper than literal fact or history, pointing toward feelings we couldn't express, even to ourselves, in any other way.

Memory is a lie, too, a creative re-creation, weaving stored elements into new patterns. The patterns we weave, and the tapestries we hold onto, tell us much about ourselves, if we care to listen.

Dreams and memories are as vivid, as real, as "real" life, and so they deceive us into believing in their literal truth. But they aren't truth. They are the lies we tell ourselves.

In a sense, life itself is a lie. We don't passively accept our experiences. We process them, passing them through screens and filters of expectation, based on past experience, on the patterns we've learned, on our need to have life be a certain way and no other. No two of us ever see things in the same way. Just ask the six eyewitnesses to the auto accident. You'll get one accident but six experiences, six realities, six lies.

Writing Lies to Reach the Deeper Truth

Sensing all this, the master writer abandons literal truth and reverts to a childlike elasticity with truth, selecting and shaping the elements of life to make the story work, to tell the more important truths that Faulkner called the truths of "the human heart in conflict with itself."

"There's how it got done and then there's how it got told," T.R. Pearson writes in *The Last of How It Was*, "and it isn't but sometimes that a thing gets done like it needs to get told."

Ben Logan's first novel, *The Land Remembers*, centers on a young man growing up on "Seldom Seen" farm in southwestern Wisconsin. The story is surely based on Logan's own childhood. And yet, Logan says, the novel is not autobiographical. "I was writing pieces of my life," he says, "but they were being arranged by an adult. . . . I was trying to cope with things I knew had meaning even if I didn't understand what it was.

"Memory has no chronology," he says. "I wander freely through the layers of time."

He wanders, he says, to achieve "feeling-level truth."

Fine for fiction writers. But what about the journalist and the how-to writer? Don't they have to stick to absolute standards of truth?

Writing Lies to Achieve Fairness

Horace Greeley listed the three cardinal rules of newswriting as: 1) accuracy; 2) accuracy; 3) accuracy. The first rule of reporting is "if your mother says she loves you, get a second source." Assume nothing. Verify everything. Don't write it unless you know it's fact. You just can't make the stuff up.

But the master nonfiction writer lies, too.

The school board meets for two hours and twenty minutes. Much of what they discuss seems trivial to the reporter ("the minutes were approved as read," "the agenda was approved as distributed," "coffee and rolls were served"), and so she leaves it out of her story.

She arranges the remaining elements to put the most important information first, shifting the argument over budget cuts and teacher firings to the top of her story, even though the board buried it at the end of the agenda.

She chooses one word, "discussion," over another word, "argument," and thus shapes the readers' response to the event.

The "discussion" turns ugly. One board member strikes another. What verb does the reporter choose—"slaps" or "slugs," "punches" or "pushes"? It makes a big difference, and she has to call it something.

Which verb contains the truth? If she chooses her verb because she believes it to be accurate and for no other reason, then she told the truth. But if we mean by telling the truth that she represented reality in a manner that is verifiably correct and subject to no other interpretation, then she didn't tell the truth, and so she must have lied.

There is no "objectivity." The master reporter can only hope and must always struggle to be fair.

Telling Truth by Telling Specifics

Covering school boards can be tough. Writing obituaries can be even tougher. How do you summarize a person's life and death, without slipping into the trite formulas repeated in so many other obituaries? Everyone "passes away after a courageous fight against a long illness." We mean such words to be a tribute, but people are worth more than a formula. No two people are truly alike, not in their living or their dying, and so no two obituaries should be alike.

To tell the kind of truth an obituary demands, you must discard tired, safe formulas and draw instead on your child's spontaneous knack for saying what is most true, most important.

The Guntersville, Alabama, *Advertiser-Gleam* consistently runs the finest obituaries I have read anywhere. Here are a few leads from *A-G* obits:

Ott Suttles

One of the whittlers outside the Courthouse, who had almost perfect attendance until he got sick about five weeks ago, Arthur (Ott) Suttles died Saturday in the Guntersville Hospital. He had been in the hospital a little more than a week. He was 85.

Mrs. Oran Clay

Although she taught school nearly half a century, the most unusual thing about Mrs. Vivian Dollie Walls Clay was her love of baseball. She went to New York to see her favorite team, the Yankees. She went to Cincinnati for a World Series. She went to Atlanta once a year for eighteen years to watch the Braves, and she saw Hank Aaron break Babe Ruth's home run record.

Pop Murphy

Twenty-three days after the death of his daughter, James Grover (Pop) Murphy had a heart attack in another daughter's car and died a short time later.

Each obit is specific in its detail. In that way, it renders truth and evokes emotion. Have editors Sam and Porter Harvey somehow insulted or trivialized the lives they write about by talking about mundane realities like baseball and whittling? On the contrary, they have exalted their subjects by focusing on what is unique about them.

Words *Can* Express How You Feel

You may never have to write an obituary, but you may have had to write a letter of condolence to a friend who has just lost a loved one. If so, you know how elusive the right words can be. How can you express your sympathy, your empathy, your willingness to help, without resorting to the tired clichés that fail so miserably to convey your true concern?

You might be tempted to write "I know how you feel," but you really don't. You can imagine how you'd feel in a similar circumstance, but you can't know how this particular individual is responding to this particular life event.

You might also be tempted to write "words cannot express how

I feel," but that would be a lie, maybe the worst lie a writer can tell. Words cannot *easily* express how you feel. Trying to find the right words may take tremendous effort and courage. You must allow yourself to feel what you feel and then admit to having felt it.

Words may not be able to *directly* express how you feel — at least not without sounding trite and corny. But the words are there if you search for them, in the language of indirect expression, of metaphor and image.

When the poet writes of love, Archibald MacLeish shows in the poem "Ars Poetica," she uses specific images rather than generalities, writing of "the leaning grasses and two lights above the sea." After all, MacLeish concludes, "A poem should not mean / but be."

" 'Love' is a word with no love in it," poet Donald Hall notes. " 'Cool thighs,' 'long hair' — these are phrases that might begin to contain love or erotic feeling."

What words and images should you pick to express your feelings? Again, you'll need to call on your spontaneous child for help. If you like, try it right now. Write "freedom" in the middle of a page in your notebook. Then write whatever words "freedom" makes you think of. Just put them anywhere on the page. Don't hold back, don't censor yourself, don't worry about making sense, and don't write what you think you "should" write. Like a child, allow yourself to respond spontaneously, openly.

Now circle all the tangible nouns on the page, things you can see or smell or take a bite out of. Using one or more of these nouns, write a paragraph or two expressing "freedom." But don't use the word "freedom" or any abstract synonym ("liberty"). Try to render "freedom" in specific images. You'll create a representation, a picture of freedom that is true to your feelings.

If you like, show your paragraphs to someone else to see if they "get it." After they read your words, do they say "freedom"? Better yet, do they *feel* it?

■■■■■■■■■■■■■■■■■■■

Exploration: A Time of Splendor in the Grass

 Think about those times in your life when you acted totally spontaneously, without regard for consequences. Make a list of as many of those times as you can remember in ten or fifteen minutes. Then continue to add to your list, jotting down life events as they occur to you, for another day or two.

Set your list aside and come back to it later. Separate your entries into "childhood" and "adult" experiences. Which list is longer? Why? What is the most recent entry on your "adult" list? How far back did you have to search for a totally spontaneous experience? When you compare the entries on the two lists, do you find anything in common? Did the same person live both sets of experiences?

Select an experience from either list and write a narration of that experience. Choose first or third person, past or present tense, whatever seems most comfortable and natural. If you let it, the experience will tell you what form it needs to take.

Here's one of mine, written in Fenner's Cafe, Darlington, Wisconsin, on my way back from a workshop on designing effective brochures.

The Hilltop, the Barclay and the YMCA

I suppose flying from California to New York City to visit a young lady I wasn't even all that sure liked me much — spending myself down below the cost of a return ticket in the process — was pretty spontaneous, if by "spontaneous" we mean "plumb dumb."

But I did have to buy a plane ticket in advance, which took some planning. And I did have to endure my mother's frequent and vehement assurances that I would be assaulted the moment I stepped off the plane and into Sin City. That took some considerable spontaneity out of the whole adventure.

I had no plan or even a clue of a plan as to what I'd do when I got there. That's pretty spontaneous (as in "plumb dumb").

The young lady, Ellen Malloy (who would in a couple of years become Ellen Cook) drank beers with me at a bar called The Hilltop, near her medieval fortress of a women's college. Frank Sinatra kept singing, "When I was twenty-one, it was a very good year." The song still goes right through me.

We took the train to the City That Never Sleeps, gave ourselves a self-gawking tour, sat in the balcony of a down-

town movie house sipping Southern Comfort and watching
Our Man Flint.

I walked her to the ultra-snooty, ultra-expensive Hotel
Barclay—Manhattanville women stay at the Barclay, don't
you know?—left Ellen with the caged birds in the lobby
and hit the street, suitcase in hand, a few bucks in my jeans,
and no place to stay, in the middle of the night in the middle
of the mean streets of New York City.

Hadn't occurred to me to make a room reservation. Just
hadn't thought about that yet. Spontaneous. Plumb dumb.
Maybe even flat-out crazy. And maybe Mama was right.

I walked a few blocks and stuck my head in at one place
that said it was a hotel. It was a stairway and a husk of a
man sitting behind a desk. I think they charged by the hour,
sheets optional. I beat it out of there, feeling pretty bad
about the world in general and not liking my chances in
particular.

A man approached. He eyed me. I figured I was dead.

"Need a place to stay?"

Say *no*. "Yeah."

The man smiled. The face of death became a human
face. "Go down two blocks and take a left. There's a Y."

And there was. I rented a bed-with-skin of a room for
six bucks a night and kept the door locked. But I was clean
and relatively safe, and I lived to write this remembrance.

Ellen and I got married and have stayed that way, an act
that has combined a great deal of spontaneity and no small
amount of planning.

Set your narration aside. When you go back to read what
you've written, how do you feel about the experience? Would
you change your actions in any way if you could? What can
this experience teach you about your writing?

As you explore all the wonderful experiences in your memory, you'll find vivid incidents waiting to be re-created. And
as you revisit your most spontaneous moments, you'll touch
the child within you. You'll call on that child to help you use
spontaneity in your writing. Your child will help you take the
risks you must take to write with originality and power.

9

Losing Track of Time

So what if it takes us a long time to write a poem? What
are we living for anyway?
— *Donald Hall*

Children live in a different time zone from the rest of us. They're
ready to get up before sunrise, hungry between meals, never sleepy
at bedtime. When it's playtime, they lose all track of time.

I remember the endless Southern California summer evenings of
my childhood. The gang would meet in the street after dinner to
play "kick the can" and "hide and seek" through the lingering sunset
and into the night, until the voices of our parents sliced through the
wonderful terror of darkness, commanding us home. For all we
knew, we could have been playing for four minutes or four hours.
There was only now.

The Hopi language has no word for "tomorrow" but many subtle
shades of "now." Sometimes I envy the Hopi.

Doing It Over—and Over and Over

Kids don't know much about scheduling their time, and they don't
have much of a concept of wasting time, either.

For example, as any parent knows, little kids want their favorite
books read to them more than once—often more than once a night.
A real time-waster for an adult, but pure pleasure for the kid. And
don't you dare try to skip a page or two, figuring the kid will never
notice. They'll notice. When Jeremiah was young, Ellen and I read
Horton Hatches the Egg, *Ferdinand* and *In the Night Kitchen* so many

times, we had them memorized. Still do, actually. Fortunately, these are great books and hold up quite well under repeated readings.

Adults take speed-reading courses to teach them how to paw pages, absorb key words and phrases at breakneck speeds, much too fast to step back ("regress") — or to savor the sound or ponder the meaning of what we've "read."

Kids' play tends to be as repetitious as their taste in reading matter. They play the same games, assume the same roles, chant the same songs, even repeat the same arguments, for hours, days, weeks. Then one day the game is gone, replaced by another.

Adults have no time to do it over. We make "to do" lists of all we feel we must do that day. When an item receives its check, it's finished. On a really bad day, I'll include two or three things I've already done ("eat breakfast," "feed the dog"), just so I can cross them off.

Sometimes even a vacation, which is supposed to be fun, can become a series of chores to be ticked off a list.

• Shopped at Wall Drug — check.
• Drove through the Badlands — check.
• Saw Mount Rushmore — check.

No need to linger. We've "done" South Dakota.

We may try to approach our writing that way, too. Write the lead, the scene, the chapter and get on to the next. We mustn't waste time, after all. How will we ever accomplish our goals, if we redo what has already been checked off the list?

The master writer, like the child, knows the satisfaction and the value in repetition. She'll write and rewrite, create and re-create, not simply revising what she's written, but searching for a different angle, looking for a nuance of meaning, a possibility of perspective, that she can only discover by writing her way into it.

Revisiting Old Friends

Ellen taught me the value of rereading a favorite book. I noticed her rereading James Agee's *A Death in the Family* and asked her why. She told me she encounters a different book each time she reads it. I tried rereading William Faulkner's *The Sound and the Fury* and found it entirely different from the book I read as a junior in college. I didn't understand the book either time, mind you, but I found something compelling and enriching both times, nevertheless. Now

I make a point of going back and revisiting old friends like Faulkner, Flannery O'Connor, Larry McMurtry and Ken Kesey from time to time. A classic like *Huckleberry Finn*, which I first met as a "children's book" now yields new riches as a book for adults to ponder.

Go back to a book you enjoyed and read it again. In what way is the book the same as when you first encountered it? In what way has it somehow changed while you weren't looking?

Go back to a story, an article, an essay, or a poem you wrote long ago. Reread it, set it aside and, without looking back, write it anew. Don't revise the old one. Create a completely new version. Then compare your two efforts. How have theme and style changed? Did you repeat any key phrases or transitions word-for-word? Was the writing really finished the first time? Is it ever finished?

By re-creating a writing you thought you had finished, you'll teach yourself to seek new approaches in everything you write. By keeping open to the possibilities for as long as you can, you'll give your writing new scope and depth.

You will, that is, if you take the time.

Converting Time-Anxiety Into Energy

Kids have time. Adults have anxiety about time. Kids get bored. Adults get crazy. Kids soar because they aren't tied down. Adults carry the weight of the world and may barely have the energy to drag themselves out of bed in the morning.

"If only I knew then what I know now," we say, meaning that if we had the experience of an adult and the time and energy of a child, we could whip the world. With zest and time plus wisdom, who could stop us?

The movie *Big* reversed that equation, showing us what might happen if a child became trapped in an adult's body. Actor Tom Hanks did a beautiful job of bringing the energy, exuberance and naiveté of a child to adult encounters, even asking a sexy woman if she wanted to "sleep over" and then claiming the top bunk.

The Hanks character eventually becomes a successful executive for a toy company. He's able to anticipate what a child will want to play with, of course, because inside he is a child. And because he's a child, he's willing to say exactly what he thinks.

The trouble is, thrust into the adult world, the child inside quickly grows up and starts getting stressed out like the rest of us.

Can we carry the zest and the energy of a child into the time-dominated world of the adult?

"I Have Measured Out My Life With Coffee Spoons"

We've been ruined by Walt Disney time-lapse photography. The flower thrusts up from the ground, the bud emerges, ripens, bursts into bloom, all in a few seconds, while the narrator explains the mystery. We break for commercial.

Nature's not like that. It takes a lot of slow to grow. Flowers unfold gently, imperceptibly. You have to be there, to put in the time, if you want to observe the miracle.

We've been ruined by the VCR and the remote control. We fast-forward through the slow spots, zap the commercials, graze from station to station. If the story doesn't grab us, we flee to another.

We've been ruined by situation comedies that resolve every problem in twenty-eight minutes and by news programs that squeeze the events of the planet into that same twenty-eight-minute frame and reduce every utterance to a seven-second sound bite.

We've been ruined by newspapers that break stories into briefs and sentences into fragments, based on the self-fulfilling prophecy of the short attention span.

We are the next generation after "instant gratification," and instant isn't fast enough anymore. We got fast, and we want faster. The technology that was supposed to liberate us has only increased our expectations of how much we should be able to accomplish in a day.

We've lost the wisdom of the philosopher who complained: "The hurrieder I go, the behinder I get."

We've lost the ability to lose ourselves in time. We take seminars to learn to "manage" time. We equate time with money. We speak of "saving time" and spending "quality time." We "sell time" on radio and television. We awaken to an alarm, strap a watch to our wrists and spend the rest of the day trying to keep to a schedule — our own if we're lucky, someone else's if we're not so lucky.

This isn't all bad. Type-A movers get a lot done, and they tend to keep those around them on task, too. But if we bring a rigid sense of time management to our writing sessions, we risk binding our creativity and even creating a block. Instead of listening to the inner voice of inspiration, we hear the clock ticking. Every second we aren't creating something "useful" or "important" moves us one second closer to the time when we must stop writing and go on to the next activity on the schedule. And what will we have to show for it? How will we prove that we were productive?

The Invention of Time

Humankind spent most of its existence without any way to measure time. Folks ate when they were hungry, slept when it got dark, got up when it got light again. Only the invention of the mechanical clock in the late thirteenth century separated time from the natural cycles of nature.

Imagine a time before there were hours and minutes and seconds. What would that timeless time have been like?

The notion of an hour wasn't invented until the thirteenth century, the minute and the second not until the seventeenth century, largely to serve the needs of capitalism and commerce. We've continued to speed up time ever since. With the invention of the cesium clock, we can keep time to an accuracy of one second every 150,000 years. Who could possibly need to measure time that accurately?

Before the fourteenth century, the length of an hour varied with the time of year. A daylight hour didn't necessarily equal a nighttime hour. We had no "standard time" until the Royal Observatory at Greenwich set the standard in 1675. In 1885, the division of the globe into time zones resulted in the invention of jet lag (known officially as "flight dysrhythmia").

We imagine time to be linear and progressive, with a past, a present and a future. But most of the world's cultures have seen time as cyclical and organic.

Newton posited that time was absolute and unchanging, but Einstein taught us that we don't all necessarily experience the same time. Since our ways of measuring time are affected by gravity, for example, time seems to go faster on the mountain top than it does by the seashore. Which time is "right?"

When we look into the skies, we are looking at history. A beam of light takes eight minutes to reach us from the sun, tens of thousands of years to get here from the Milky Way, two and one-half million years to make the trek from the Andromeda Galaxy. So which "time" are we seeing? What does "now" mean in this context?

Capturing Time and Letting Time Go

In my first book for Writer's Digest Books, *Freeing Your Creativity: A Writer's Guide*, I spent a chapter talking about ways to make time for our writing. I maintained then, and I still believe, that we must *make* the time. No one will give it to us, and we'll never find it. I wrote about making writing appointments and then keeping those appointments, come fire, flood or famine. I also maintained then, and still believe, that we may have to be fairly ruthless about all this. If we want and need to write, if we want to utter that breathless "yes" to our creative selves, we must say "no" to other things.

But the way you handle that time after you've made it can be crucial to the writing you create and the way you feel about that writing. Let's begin to get back in touch with our childhood sense of timelessness with a couple of reflections.

A Day Without a Schedule

Suppose you could step out of time and spend a day totally as you wished, without schedules or obligations. You wouldn't *have* to do anything. What would that day look like? Spend a few minutes (see—there's that business of spending time again) imagining such a day and, if you like, write a paragraph or two describing that day and how it feels.

Would you sleep the day away? Would you read for hours? Would you sit in a chair and simply stare until the urge to stop sitting and staring compelled you to get up? How long would that take? What would make you move?

How many such free days would it take before you became tired of doing what you were doing or not doing what you weren't doing? I've heard many retirees say that they got caught up on their reading and napping and even their golfing and their gardening a lot faster than they imagined. They soon sought out new interests, including volunteer service and educational projects, to maintain their sense of worth and satisfaction.

I suspect that my free day would be as full of activity as any other day. I have no gift for sitting and staring, and forcing myself to do so would be torture. For me, the key would be in making possibilities instead of plans and in fighting off the compulsion to make a mental list and then driving myself until I had checked every item off the list.

Entering the Timeless Zone

We'll probably never escape schedules, even in retirement. And many of us will have to be somewhat rigid about building writing time into our daily lives to be able to write at all. But when she reaches her writing time, the master empties herself of all time-awareness. Time, after all, is simply another trick, another temptation to get us to think about ourselves instead of about the writing. The master nurtures and cultivates her childlike ability to live in a timeless state of creation, fully, intensely alive to the moment and to the creation and to nothing else.

If you can create large blocks of time for writing, well and good. But you may have to learn to relax, breathe deeply and plunge into the Timeless Zone for fifteen or twenty minutes, if that's all the time you can make. Whatever the duration, you must strip away excuses and evasions and fall into the writing.

Whatever you do, you must not spend any of your time worrying about writing, worrying about how much or how little or how good or how bad, or worrying about not writing. Worrying about writing is not writing. Only writing is writing.

■ ■ ■ ■ ■ ■ ■ ■ ■ ■ ■ ■ ■ ■ ■ ■ ■ ■ ■
Exploration: Reliving
a Timeless Time

 Recall an occasion during which you lost all track of time. Write a description of where you were and what you were doing. Set your description aside for a day or two, and then come back to it and try to understand how this suspension of time occurred. Could you structure — or unstructure — your writing time so that you could recapture this sense of timeless-ness? What would that look and feel like? What would your writing gain if you could?

For me, reading a good book will sometimes lead me into the Timeless Zone, but with other books I wind up checking the clock constantly and counting the number of pages until the end of the chapter.

I can often suspend my sense of time while running, but never while swimming and seldom while riding an exercise bicycle.

Sitting in the sunshine with a baseball game spread out in

front of me often makes the clock go away—unless I get to worrying about Where I Ought to Be and What I Ought to Be Doing.

Have you ever lost track of time while you were writing? How did that happen? Could you let it happen again?

By recapturing an occasion of timelessness in your life, you're getting back in touch with your inherent ability to become absorbed in the task. If, as you write, you feel yourself dominated by time, go back in your mind to that occasion when time was suspended for you. If you find yourself backsliding into clock-watching, gently nudge yourself and keep writing. But don't get angry with yourself. You're not bad for "failing." You're only a time-bound human like the rest of us, and you're battling years of training to become a dedicated clock-watcher.

With practice, you can learn to suspend your sense of time while you write. When you do, you'll have freed the full power and intensity of your concentration for your writing.

Here's my exploration of a recent timeless time.

The Dock at Teal Lake

Ellen and I bring our chairs out on the dock to watch the sunset. We have left our watches in the cabin. Only the sinking sun, the deepening colors of the clouds, and the gathering darkness mark the passage of time, and I lack the art, thank God, of translating this passage into hours, minutes and seconds.

A mother duck and her eight babies glide silently into our cove. They bob along the bank, looking for a night's lodging, or so I imagine.

A beaver pushes into view, at first just a head with "V" of water behind. As she gets closer, we can see her sleek rat body. She circles in front of our dock, haahing her outrage at our presence. Beavers have their babies early in the season. We're probably close to her lodge, and she wants us to go away.

Dragonflies mate on a lily pad. A loon calls in the distance. Gradually, gently, the urge to Do Something subsides. The internal clamoring becomes absorbed into the silent sliding of ducks through sunset waters. Soul breathes slowly.

I think about our canoe trip earlier in the day. We paddled through liquid silence. A turtle, sunning itself on a log, sensed our approach and plopped into the water. A loon floated low in the water, dove for an improbably long time, finally resurfaced. A blue heron tiptoed on spindly jointed legs, took off with stunning grace, borne on impossibly large wings.

The sunset will not be rushed. It doesn't demand that we stay and partake. It only presents itself. There has never been another like it. There will never be another like it. It will exist only in this moment. There can be no coming back later for a replay.

10

Play-Acting

Know thyself.
— *Plutarch*
Then try to forget it.
— *George V. Higgins*

When I was young, I wore a pair of six-shooters strapped to my hips from the time I got up until the time I went to bed. (I grew up to be a pacifist. Go figure.) I was Wild Bill Hickok (Guy Madison's sanitized television version of him, anyway), Hopalong Cassidy, The Lone Ranger, Davy Crockett.

Then I was Superman, Captain Marvel or even Mighty Mouse, racing around the yard with a bath towel cape trailing behind me — but in my mind I was soaring through the clouds.

When I got a little older, I was Frank Hardy, and my best friend, Craig Marvel, was brother Joe. We burrowed through storm drains and neighbors' garages, looking for clues to the mysteries we concocted.

Then I became Jerry West sinking the game-winning jump shot, Sandy Koufax gunning a fastball past Willie McCovey, Jon Arnett threading through would-be tacklers for another Ram touchdown.

I spent hours watching and then emulating my heroes. And during the whole course of my growing up, I was covertly watching my father, my first and best hero, learning from him how to be a man.

Now kids are more likely to be Teenage Mutant Ninja Turtles than cowboys, but the nature of the game remains the same. A child doesn't play at being the hero. She *becomes* the hero.

A few of us achieve fame by continuing to play-act after we grow up. Comedians such as Robin Williams, Jonathan Winters, Lily

Tomlin and Whoopie Goldberg are incredibly adept at slipping in and out of diverse and hilarious characters. An actor with the skill of a Dustin Hoffman can become in turn Lenny Bruce, Willie Loman, Tootsie and Raymond Babbitt.

The rest of us do a bit of acting, too. Our work selves are likely to be quite different from our at-home selves. The face we show to the world is probably more studied, more reserved, than the face we share with loved ones. But there's little fun in this kind of play-acting. We've learned to adapt and survive by "acting our age," which generally means suppressing a lot of natural impulses and passing up a lot of potential fun.

Losing Your Shadow Selves

The longer you put on your public self, the more solidified and unchangeable it becomes. Your other selves, the people you might have been, don't go away. They slip into shadow, beyond conscious awareness, and remain as unexplored possibilities.

In the movie *Thelma and Louise*, the character played by Susan Sarandon is fond of saying, "You get what you settle for." She might have gone a step further: You *are* what you settle for.

Can you map the road you've traveled in becoming the self you are now? Only in retrospect can you see the crossroads and begin to understand the consequences of your choices. The man or woman you married, or didn't marry, the job you took and the job that job led you to, the city or town or countryside you settled in or refused to get tied to—these choices and others create, define and limit you.

So many of the important influences in our lives come to us almost randomly. How did you meet the man or woman who became your mate? How easily would it have been for you never to have met at all?

We define ourselves, too, by our many smaller choices. Folks are Sears people or Penneys people, Ford folk or Chevy folk, with onion or without onion, pickup truck with gun rack or Honda Prelude with bike rack. If we aren't careful, our possessions can own us, stereotyping us not only in the eyes of others but in our own.

We "other" others. "I could never be like that," we say both of the Hitler and of the Christ, thus freeing ourselves from the responsibility for evil and from the struggle to be better than we are. Such othering is a delusion. "Nothing that is human is foreign to me," as San Francisco *Chronicle* columnist Charles McCabe was fond of saying.

Calling Down to Central Casting

You are potentially many. You must struggle against the pressure to be only one. The master writer draws on her shadow selves, becoming a character as she writes, putting on that person's skin, feeling her feelings and thinking her thoughts, because those feelings and thoughts are a part of her, too.

It's as if she calls down to some internal "central casting," bringing up a character and letting that character take the stage. There is no thought, then, of "self-expression" when the master creates. She is allowing the other to express itself through the writing. Writing for the master becomes a matter of getting out of the way.

"As for characters, they are all invented," says playwright August Wilson (*The Piano Lesson, Two Trains Running*). "At the same time, they are all made up out of myself. So they're all me, different aspects of my personality, I guess. . . . I write different parts of myself and I try to invent or discover some other parts."

Hearing Voices

Your writing has a voice, a personality. It may vary from piece to piece, audience to audience. The voice that speaks words of endearment in a love letter is surely different from the voice that advises your coworkers in a memo that you'll be leaving for vacation Friday.

Each voice is a variant on your "natural" voice, a product of the way you observe and think and express your thoughts and observations. Even when you write from a shadow self, one of the many possible selves inside you that hardly ever gets expressed, your writing is authentically you and nobody else.

I borrow voices that I like, if they serve my need. But they go through me and are mine, are me. Most of the time the voice sounds like the voice I hear when I think. But sometimes it sounds like Willard Scott, the NBC weatherman, or Mick Belker, one of the cops on the old "Hill Street Blues" program. Sometimes I sound the way T.R. Pearson sounds in my head when I read his novels. Sometimes I sound like the Walt Disney narrator in all those "True Life Adventures." When I sound like that, I know I need to do some heavy rewriting. Pretty ponderous, that True Life narrator.

Playwright Terrence McNally (*Lips Together, Teeth Apart*) hears voices when he writes, too, the voices of the actors he hopes will inhabit the roles he is creating.

"When you tell someone you've written a part for a specific actor," McNally wrote in the *New York Times*, "they often assume the part is about or based on that actor's personal life. . . . Nothing could be further from the truth. When you write for an actor, it is because you hear their voice in your head, see their faces and gestures as you create characters that are your own personal devils or angels. . . .

"Great actors make me want to write for them. I hear their voices when I'm creating a character. I see their faces and body language when I try to imagine how that character is behaving."

Do you "cast" actors, or colleagues, friends or family members in "roles" when you write? If it helps you to create an authentic character, a being of complexity and contradiction, then cast away, and don't worry too much about offending the family member or friend you're using as your model. Since you're writing from your personal perception of that person, chances are your models won't recognize themselves in your portraits.

■ ■ ■ ■ ■ ■ ■ ■ ■ ■ ■ ■ ■ ■ ■ ■
Exploration: Getting Inside the Other

 Assume the part of a character—either a real or fictional person—and make a journal entry *as* that character. Don't write about the character. *Be* the character. Think as she thinks. Feel as she feels. Make it a long enough journal entry to really experience this other self.

This sort of exploration will strengthen you as a writer of both fiction and nonfiction, for in either sort of writing, the people you write about become "characters."

Gradually you'll cease writing *about* these characters and will begin to write *as* them. At that point, they'll begin to stand up and cast their own shadows, as Faulkner once said, and the reader will believe in their reality.

They may even hijack "your" writing and take it where they need it to go. Let them. It's their story now.

Here are a few of my journal entries, written as other people.

Put Away Your Sword

They will kill him for certain now. Perhaps they already have.

Why didn't he fight? We would have fought with him, died for him, if need be. It isn't a question of courage. Didn't I stand with him through everything? Didn't I draw my sword when the soldiers came?

"Put away your sword," he said, looking at me with those eyes that see right through a man and into his soul. It's as if he wanted to die. Maybe he had given up after all.

What good would it have done to tell those fools that I was with him? Would it help him now if I died with him? He wouldn't want that. Didn't he tell me I'd do what I did? He knew. He always knew.

He has left me with nothing but questions. And this ache, this longing, this loneliness. To hell with causes. I love him, and he's gone. What cause could be worth his precious life? If he were here, he would chide me and explain things, show me how it all had to be the way it is. He'd make this ache go away. He'd stretch out his hand to me, and I'd grasp it, and the storm inside me would subside.

Or maybe I'd never understand. But understanding wouldn't matter.

What now? Back to our nets? Back to the life we knew before he came? He has changed everything. How could we ever go back?

I love him. It all comes down to that. Not kingdoms springing from mustard seeds. Not faith moving mountains. Just love. I can't imagine life without him now.

This is, of course, Simon Peter, the night he denied Christ three times.

Riding That Lightning for a While

It happened again today. It's really kind of funny, if you look at it right.

The owners all know who I am—or was—of course. Hell, that's probably why I got my foot in the door and my hat on the table in the first place. But after that, it was up to me. Nothing you done in the past can help you sell the product line today.

But now and again there'll be a customer in the store who'll overhear somebody call my name, and they'll look at me funny and start to grin and nod.

"You're him, aren't you," this fella says today, like he was telling me an important piece of news I might have missed. He waddles over and sticks out a big wet hand for shaking.

"By *Gawd*," he says. Then he says, "It *is* you, ain't it?"

"It's me," I say, and he grins and nods some more. "I knew it was you," he says, and he asks me to sign the back of a receipt from the U-Pump. I sign it.

"For the kid," he says. Like my name would mean anything to his kid. He just stands there, grinning, maybe trying to think of something else to say, while I try to convince Roy Earl Roth to carry more of my high-end sippin' whiskey and less of the other fella's high-end sippin' whiskey.

"You must miss it, huh?" the fella blurts out.

"No, not really," I tell him. Does he think I've been sitting around, looking at scrapbooks these past thirty-four years?

He follows me out, and I think for a minute he might climb right into the car with me, but he doesn't. I watch him out of the rearview, and he just stands there, looking after the car, a big, moony grin on his face.

It set me to thinking about that year—not in a hangdog way, like I wished I could be back there doing it all over again. It was more like remembering a movie you saw a long time ago, a real exciting picture that you liked a lot, but when the credits roll and the lights come up, you blink your eyes and grab your hat and go out into the sunshine and get on with your life.

Folks say aren't you sad? or aren't you bitter? or what the hell happened to you after that? But I *had* that one year. If Billy Bruton hadn't of got injured, I might never of got the chance to do what I done at all. That's the thing. How many folks ever get to do something like that? *Damn* few. Would it have been any sweeter if I'd of had twenty years of glory instead of just one?

It was time to get on with my life, and I got on with it. It would of had to happen sometime. While I was riding that lightning bolt — with the crowds screaming for me, and my teammates pounding me on the back — I wasn't thinking about next year or the year after that. I was just giving it one hell of a ride while it lasted.

You can't go to comparing, not and stay sane, you can't. The only day you got is today. I was doing what I love, having the time of my life doing it. I still am. I got my family. I got this beautiful Carolina country to drive around in. I do a little hunting, a little fishing. I'm a happy man.

Folks will tell you Ted Williams was the last man to hit over .400 in the big leagues. But you know better, don't you?

I wrote this as Bob "Hurricane" Hazel, who got called up to the Milwaukee Braves in mid-season of 1957 and led them to a pennant and a World Series win over the New York Yankees.

Man Will Not Simply Endure

You don't do it for the awards, which you have no right to expect and which, if they do come, can serve in no sense as validation or vindication for the sweat and the labor.

I have endured ridicule and, worse than ridicule, indifference, have bared my heart and felt the soul-numbing indifference of the world that continues on as if I had never written, had never shouted my puny "I am" into the abyss.

Now they wish to honor me, to honor my work, work that they have called obscure and obscene. I do not believe that I am bitter, do not believe I have let bitterness enter into the deepest realms of not-consciousness, something beneath and deeper and stronger than consciousness, although the bitterness may have infected me without my being aware of it, in the way we can consciously deny our deepest truths, our very natures, and insist on the flimsy fictions we create to wear for others and which we ultimately come to believe in ourselves, even if no one else is fooled by them.

What wisdom can they expect now, that I haven't already said in the work? I keep coming back to an image. A man, pale, skinny, naked, a poor animal, stands alone on a shelf of rock overlooking a deep valley. A violent storm rages all around him. Next moment he may be crushed, may be struck down by an awesome power awesomely indifferent to his existence. And he knows it, knows it in the depths of his frightened heart, and yet, knowing it, from the very depths of this knowing, he raises a skinny naked arm and forms a fist to shake in defiance at the forces that might next moment sweep him away like so much dust.

The storm passes, and he is standing still on that shelf of rock, having not merely endured but somehow in his proud, foolish, insane defiance, having prevailed.

You may have figured out by the length of the sentences alone that this is my attempt at being William Faulkner, working himself up to his acceptance speech for the Nobel Prize.

I Gotta Get Out of This Place

"Hell, honey. I understand just how you feel," Ott said when I came for refills. "Men get periods, too. Mine's February."

That set all the old wheezers in their bib overalls and their seed caps to howling.

But even old Ott could see I wasn't right, even though I hadn't said or done anything different. Maybe that's the problem right there, that it's been too long since I've said or done anything different than poured coffee and brought big scrambles with hash browns, laughed at lame jokes and fended off hands whose owners have pretty much forgotten what the patting and pinching is supposed to be all about anyway.

Maybe it takes an aimless man to notice, not having much else on his mind but whether to go down to Sid Neely's barbershop to shoot the breeze or over to the courthouse square to sit and whittle or maybe down to the river to hunker down with the fishermen and not-fish for a while.

What Ott said made me know I'd gotten back into my pit again, not what he said, exactly, but the fact that I had to go on back to the kitchen to get another pot of coffee brewing and to fetch a box of beef patties from the freezer to set out to thaw for the lunch crowd, even though those things could have waited. I needed to get away from Ott and the rest and their harmless guffaws and the hands that didn't really remember what they're fumbling for. I usually don't even mind the teasing.

I realized then that I hadn't been enjoying that first cup of coffee or the crossword puzzle or the cool feel of the pie dough in my hands or any of the other little things that usually makes life seem good. All those things turn on you when you feel bad. They make you feel small, like you should be wanting something more with your life than just pouring coffee and shoveling hash browns and big scrambles and cowboy omelets into old men who don't even take time to chew, let alone taste.

I gotta get out of this place. Like that time I drove to Madison and wandered around on State Street, feeling lonely, but good lonely. I walked all the way out along the lake path and back through the student union, with all the smoke and noise and not a soul knowing or caring who I was, and it wasn't until I was almost back to the car that I started worrying about the cafe and the chores that weren't getting done—as if the world couldn't get along without me for a day.

Yeah. I gotta get out of here. Maybe for more than just a day.

You've just met Billie Jo Ferken, a character in the novel I'm working on called *The Year of the Buffalo*. As you've seen, she's gotta get out of there.

Rosie's Morning

When she says "Sit!" I have to sit right where I am if I don't she pushes my hinder down and says "Good" and pats me but if I get up she says, "No" and her voice is hard but not mad she isn't mad like she gets if I run into the street but I can't remember just can't I have to chase the squirrel just have to.

When the voice comes out of the box he wakes up, he gets up and feeds me and I go back upstairs and jump on the bed and poke my nose at her and she makes the mumble noise and her hand tries to pat me. She doesn't get up he gets up right away and makes me go outside first to wet and come to the back door he waits for me and lets me in and gives me my kibbles in my bowl and lets me back outside again the grass is wet on my paws I see the squirrel and chase it to the fence and then I sit by the back fence and watch the cars.

I go back upstairs on the bed until she gets up I go downstairs and wait for him to be done in the basement I bark when the man comes and throws the paper at the house. He gets his bowl from the cupboard and gets his cereal from the cupboard and he lets me have two kibbles of cereal they are very sweet. I can watch him eat but I can't put my paws on him when he eats. He tells me "Off" but he pats me he isn't mad at me.

She gets into the car and the car drives away. He puts my toys in the pokey and he says "Pokey time" and pats me I get in the pokey and he tells me I am good and closes the gate and tells me I am good and I hear him go away and the house is quiet he is not mad at me and he comes back.

This is Ellen's dog, Rosie. Apparently, she doesn't know much about sentence structure, but what can you expect from a dog?

Eve's Tired of Taking the Blame

You don't have to limit yourself to a single character, and the play-acting doesn't have to assume the form of a journal entry.

Kate Winters, chaplain at the Catholic church on campus here in Madison, recently showed me how dynamic role-playing can be. "I kept getting nervous every time I approached the readings for today," she said of her sermon. "So I did with them the same thing I might do with a friend who was somehow unnerving me. I took them to a favorite coffee shop."

Here, in part, is how her "dialogue" with the "characters" from the day's Bible readings came out.

Eve (to Kate): All right. I'll talk. I'm tired of holding my breath and my feelings about this story.

(to Adam): You know, don't you, that ever since we blew our chance at paradise by blaming each other for eating of that special tree, I've received nothing but scorn throughout history, while you have gotten tons of sympathy for being done in by this female "temptress"? You wouldn't believe how they've blown this story out of proportion.

Adam: It's not my fault. Someone had to take the blame for the fact that we humans are mere humans and not the gods we would like to be.

Eve: Oh, Adam. There you go again. Someone always needs to take the blame! Do you know who usually gets it?

(To serpent): Hey, I'm not really talking about you. Though we both did get a bum rap from this story, didn't we? . . .

Portly scribe: I must say, I do emphathize with that woman who was tired of feeling blamed. . . . But what about us? Has anyone tried to understand the extreme pressure we were under when this man Jesus began to stir up all kinds of excitement in our community? . . . We Jews were in enough trouble already. . . . Then Jesus comes along—healing, expelling demons, gathering disciples. Can you not see what appears to be a gentle savior in your time was a frightening rabble-rousing threat in ours? . . . In your readings, we are always seen as ignorant, hard-hearted fools. . . .

Paul (to Kate): You twentieth-century women, you really misunderstand me! . . . Maybe I did go a little overboard in separating the spirit from the body . . . but my new churches needed something to look forward to. Things were awfully rough. You just don't know.

Woman of Corinth (to Kate): Watch out. He's good at guilt. . . .

"So that's what happened in the coffee shop," Kate concluded. "If the spirit lives, the conversation never ends."

And that's what can happen to us, when we allow the spirit of the "other" inside of us to be expressed in our writing.

11

Finding Writing Heroes

Shazam!
— *Magic word that transforms Billy Batson into Captain Marvel*

I didn't select my childhood heroes. They selected me. I loved them without reservation.

In absorbing the qualities of my hero, I was shaping my own values and defining myself. Davy Crockett (as played by Fess Parker in the Disney version) told me, "Be sure you're right, then go ahead," and I carried these words as my credo beyond childhood, through the tumultuous Vietnam War years and to the present day. When Superman fought his "never-ending battle for truth, justice and the American way," I imagined myself fighting for those things too, and I still do — although my definitions of what that means have changed over the years.

When I reached adolescence, I learned that having heroes wasn't permitted. Cynicism became the order of the day. I put away my coonskin cap, stored my Superman comic books, and even rejected Mom and Dad for a while.

That's healthy. Real-life heroes, unlike their comic book counterparts, are only human. We need to get some distance so we can learn to admire and respect our heroes while still being selective about their values and understanding of their limitations.

As adults, some of us wear our politically correct cynicism the way we once may have worn a cape or spurs. We reject the notion of heroes — or, at least, we say we do. But why, then, do we become so angry when we find out that John Kennedy was a womanizer or that Pete Rose couldn't say no to a bet? Disappointed, sure. But why irate? Kennedy was no more or less the president we thought him to be all along, and Pete Rose has no fewer base hits and hustled no less on the baseball field. We feel betrayed because we were secretly expecting, even demanding, that Kennedy be more than a president, Rose more than a ballplayer. We were making them into idols.

The B-Movie Cowpoke Who Became a Legend

Like a lot of other Americans, I have made a hero of John Wayne, the Great American Cowboy.

John Wayne was born Marion Michael Morrison, but the studio name brims with grit and gristle and is as subtle as a punch in the nose. Wayne starred in over two hundred films, including the lyric *The Quiet Man* and tons of war flicks. But he was most at home in the American West of myth and legend, the realm of clearly defined right and wrong, quick solutions to problems, a decisive outcome to every conflict. We know the rules in John Wayne's mythic Old West, and the good guys always win.

Wayne appeared in a slew of B-Westerns for Republic Studios before making his mark as the Ringo Kid in *Stagecoach* with the great director John Ford. Wayne dominated America's love affair with the cowboy movie for years, looming over the landscape in films like *Hondo* and *Rio Bravo*. He was the first choice to play the role of Matt Dillon when "Gunsmoke" made the jump from radio to television (producers figured the portly William Conrad, who had developed the role for radio, just wouldn't fly with TV viewers). But Wayne stepped aside in favor of his friend James Arness, whom Wayne introduced to viewers before the first episode of what became TV's longest running Western.

In the 1960s, when middle age, a bout with cancer, a recession in the film industry and the sudden ending of America's infatuation with the Western should have ended Wayne's career, he won an Academy Award for his parody of his own legend as paunchy, drunken Rooster Cogburn in *True Grit*.

By the time he bid his fans a moving farewell in *The Shootist*, in which he was gunned down, Wayne had become for many a real-life hero as well as a celluloid one. The qualities he embodied on the screen had become fused with the man himself. On screen he battled gunslingers, cattle rustlers and crooked sheriffs. Off screen, he fought Communist one-worlders, big government over-regulators, and cancer, which he called "the big C." He brought courage to all these battles.

He was outrageously conservative before it became fashionable to elect right-wing actors to high public office. He rode out isolation and ridicule with the same stoicism with which he later accepted praise.

"On screen and off, he is what he is," movie critic Richard Schickel wrote, "and he's willing to show it all to us. . . . In a world of slicksters and sharpies and smooth talkers, we are grateful to him . . . for the lessons he taught us as kids and now teaches our kids—lessons about honor, honesty, self-reliance and courage, and just being one's self, no matter what."

He remains one of my heroes.

Imitating the Writer-Hero

As writers, we may adopt writer-heroes and, quite naturally, imitate them in our own writing. My Faulkner period came hard on the heels of my Hemingway period (I almost got the bends). For a while I fancied myself the new J.D. Salinger, and then the new Kurt Vonnegut, Jr.

Gradually, through imitation and absorption of style, through acceptance of certain themes and techniques and rejection of others, I began to develop and express my own evolving style. Good thing, because no editor is looking for a bad imitation of Hemingway, and the world doesn't need a "new" anybody. It still has the work of the originals.

■ ■

Exploration: Taking on the Qualities of the Hero

 Do you have a hero-writer or perhaps some other kind of creative hero? Make a list of potential candidates.

What qualities do the people on your list share? What do these qualities tell you about your own values?

My list of writer-heroes includes Ken Kesey, Natalie Goldberg, Brenda Ueland, Cynthia Gorney, William Faulkner, Larry McMurtry, William Saroyan, Dorothea Brande, Mark Twain and Wallace Stegner.

I have lots of other creative heroes, including:

- Chuck Jones, Bob Clampett and Jay Ward, who made wonderful cartoons
- Mel Blanc, who invented over three thousand voices for the cartoons
- Stan Freberg, who makes marvelously funny ads
- Tom Lehrer, who teaches math and satire with a piano
- Katharine Hepburn, who has made terrific movies and has steadfastly refused to be anybody but herself
- John Wayne, ditto (how embarrassing for a political "liberal" to admit such a thing, but there you are)
- "Pistol" Pete Maravich and "Hot Rod" Huntley, basketball players of uncommon originality and ability
- Jay Silverheels, nee Harold J. Smith, the full-blooded Mohawk Indian who played Tonto to Clayton Moore's Lone Ranger and who founded the Indian Actors' Workshop
- Huckleberry Finn, who risked hell to save his friend Jim.

Write a paragraph or two summarizing the qualities your heroes have in common. Select one hero from your list and write several paragraphs describing this person, faults and all. Ask your hero a question that has genuinely troubled you. Assume the role of your hero and answer the question.

What does this exploration teach you about yourself and your writing? In what way are you a better writer for your encounter with your heroes? In what way are you more yourself for having tried, perhaps subconsciously, to be more like your hero?

Qualities of My Heroes

My creative heroes are 100 percent themselves. Nobody does what they do the way they do it. I could recognize their work without any bylines or other identifying labels.

Being original requires a lot of risk-taking (what we used to call courage). If it hasn't been done that way before, then we don't know for sure it will work, after all, or that it will be accepted. My heroes have staked their professional and sometimes their personal lives on their creative vision.

The risks they take are purposeful, necessary for the work they want to do or the goals they want to achieve. Evel Knievel doesn't appear on my list.

I doubt if they'd call what they do "courageous" or even talk much about the risks they take. I sense in what I've read or heard about my heroes that they do what they do because it's fun and because it seems right. I think they do it for love, and success follows.

"We're all in this to please ourselves," comic-book author Mike Baron says.

"Even if I knew nothing would emerge from the book," John Steinbeck wrote while he was working on *East of Eden*, "I would still write it."

All the people on my list are successful, though. I'm sure thousands of writers have just as much courage and vision as the ones on my list, but I've never heard of them.

I see another common thread binding the people on my list. In every case, I like what they do. I suppose I could grudgingly admire somebody whose work didn't make my soul tap in time to its beat, but I couldn't put them on my heroes list.

Crossing the Line Between the Writing and the Writer

Ken Kesey makes my list of writer-heroes for having written two of the finest novels I've ever become lost in — *One Flew Over the Cuckoo's Nest* and *Sometimes a Great Notion*.

Kesey became a public figure as well as a writer in the late sixties and early seventies. He packed the house for lectures on college campuses and then jumped into a Day-Glo painted bus with his "Merry Pranksters" and took off cross-country to discover America. The adulation and cult status he achieved must have been pretty heady stuff, but Kesey voluntarily stepped out of the spotlight, telling a groaning San Jose, California, audience that it wasn't healthy to have all that energy focused on him. He went to his brother's dairy farm in Oregon and let the world get on without his advice.

I really admire him for that. Not many have the inner peace to turn away from celebrity status.

Taking What Nurtures and Rejecting the Rest

But Kesey's life has not been entirely exemplary, in my view. He ingested a lot of mind-altering drugs, which was his business but an option I reject for myself. He also gave LSD-laced punch to a lot of unsuspecting folks. I have to get off Kesey's bus at that point, but that doesn't change my admiration for his other actions, and it doesn't prevent me from learning, growing and marveling every time I dip into the shifting stream-of-consciousness river of *Sometimes a Great Notion* or recall how McMurphy's sacrifice redeemed Chief Broom and the other inmates in *One Flew Over the Cuckoo's Nest*.

William Saroyan's personal life was by all accounts a train wreck, and according to son Aram, he wasn't the world's best father. But *A Human Comedy* still makes my heart sing, and Saroyan's short stories help me to affirm "myself upon the earth."

Saints, no. Writer-heroes, you bet—for me, anyway. You have to pick your own. That's the only way it works. Something inside you has to respond to something you perceive in the hero.

Hero worship and even conscious imitation of heroic qualities can teach you much about yourself. As you take on those qualities as a writer, you will more clearly define your own methods and goals while teaching yourself what the chosen master can show you.

The master writer dares to become her own hero. She isn't afraid to put on another writer, the way children put on a hero when they play. The master immerses herself in the hero-writer, thinking that writer's thoughts, absorbing that writer's technique. She emerges, not a clone of the hero-writer, but a more fully realized, more complete version of herself. She learns the lessons the hero-writer can teach, tests the experience she gains against her own experience and intuitions, and then defines her own style, her own craft, against her evolving standards.

■■■■■■■■■■■■■■■■■■■■■

Exploration: Remembering the Little People

 You have won the Pulitzer Prize for literature (or poetry or journalism) or even the Nobel Prize for your contributions to human progress. You will soon appear on the cover of *Time* magazine as its "Person of the Year."

Geraldo, Phil, Sally Jessy and Oprah all want you; you're holding out for Letterman.

Write that *Time* cover story. Discuss your background, the major influences on your work, and your primary contributions to our society. Have fun here. Invention is all. But, let your fanciful article be true in the sense that it is true to your heart and your ambitions, true to the writing you would really like to accomplish and the effect you would like it to have.

Write your story before reading on.

Here's an exploration from one of my current students:

A Butterfly in My Soup

Relaxing in her spacious Vermont home, Pulitzer Prize-winning novelist Amy Neuenfeldt admits she hasn't always been this content or this successful.

"Life hasn't always been easy, but I've been lucky enough to have family and friends who have supported me," Neuenfeldt said.

Neuenfeldt's critically acclaimed novel and *New York Times* best-seller, *There's a Butterfly in My Soup*, about a woman's struggle to be a singer despite her own personal adversities, was awarded a Pulitzer Prize in New York last week. Neuenfeldt also writes columns for the *New York Times* and contributes to such magazines as *New Woman*, *Glamour* and *Redbook*. She has published two other novels.

Born to Dennis and Pat Neuenfeldt in Milwaukee, Wisconsin, in 1971, Neuenfeldt was the eldest of their three daughters. Encouraged by her success in several accelerated high school English courses, Neuenfeldt became determined to develop her knack for writing.

"I always enjoyed finding clear ways to organize ideas on paper," she said. "I can remember one English teacher, Ms. Minga, who gave up countless lunch hours to go over my papers with me. I wasn't satisfied until it was perfect — or as close to perfect as I could get."

Although Neuenfeldt enjoyed writing nonfiction, she had many doubts about her ability to write fiction.

"I never considered myself creative. I would read as many books about writing as I could get my hands on, searching for inspiration, but it took me a long time to find it," she said.

Neuenfeldt said her goals became less clear when she experienced the deaths of her sister, both grandfathers and her grandmother during college.

"For many, college is a time when they are free to discover what they want to do and who they want to be," she said. "My world had been turned upside down. It took all my energy just to get through the days. I couldn't even think about the future."

It was that same experience which also made her more determined to write.

"Losing so many people who were close to me made me care even more about others," she said. "It made me realize not only how fragile life is, but how important it is that we make attempts to preserve it. If I can do that through my writing, then I've been successful."

Through her novels and her weekly column profiling individuals who have gone to great lengths to get where they are, Neuenfeldt hopes to help others believe in themselves.

"If I hadn't looked around and realized there were others struggling with many of the same things I was, I would never have survived my own tragedies," she said. "It's important to me that others feel that same sense of belonging to something greater that I did. Looking at the big picture helped restore my confidence in myself and my abilities."

From *See Spot* to *Dreams*

Amy has written an extraordinary story, one that I'm sure predicts her own emergence as a master writer. By treating herself as a writer-hero, she has clarified her goals and values as a writer.

Another student, Lynne Snifka, imagined herself having written *Rite of Way*, a book offering a new model for the American educational system. After winning her Pulitzer, Snifka opened an inner city "creativity center" in her hometown of Milwaukee. "Here kids are invited to spend time, free of charge," she wrote, "using the facility and staff to develop their own creative projects and ideas." Snifka named her center "Sam's," after one of the characters in her book.

Pamela Austin won both the Nobel and Pulitzer Prizes for *See Spot*, her series exposing the corruption in the American education system. (Are our students trying to tell us something?)

"Best-selling author and women's rights activist" Kellie Krumplitsch won a Pulitzer for her novel, *Inside the Minds of Women*, "an effort to show the setbacks and successes her gender has experienced globally over the last twenty-five years."

Having landed a job as the successor to his idol, Mike Royko, Antony Bruno won his Pulitzer for his "incessant efforts to wake up the American public" with his social commentary, *Within the Box*.

Incorporating real-life problems into romance novels earned a Pulitzer for Shoshana Kamis and her fifth novel, *Dreams*.

These are all dreams, of course, fantasies rooted as much in the child as in the emerging adult. But all our accomplishments begin as dreams such as these, and only by allowing ourselves to pursue our childish dreams will we release the master writer to do what is in her to do.

12

Learning What Can't Be Taught

Nobody can counsel and help you, nobody. There is only
one single way. Go into yourself. Search for the
reason that bids you write. . . .
— *Rainer Maria Rilke*

If you've ever enjoyed an animated cartoon, you can probably trace your pleasure to a fellow named Chuck Jones. Jones invented the Road Runner, Wile E. Coyote, Pepe LePew and other Warner Brothers cartoon characters. He was also instrumental in the development of Bugs Bunny, Daffy Duck and Elmer Fudd, and worked with Dr. Seuss to bring the Grinch and Horton to television.

In his autobiography, *Chuck Amuck*, Jones traces the origins of his interest in drawing to his father's habit of starting small businesses. Charles Jones Senior would print reams of fancy stationery for each new start-up and lay in a huge supply of Ticonderoga pencils emblazoned with the company name. When the businesses went belly up, as each invariably did, Chuck Junior would inherit the stationery and pencils, along with the admonition to "only draw on one side" to use up the offending paper faster.

Jones says he received neither undue criticism nor insincere praise from his parents for his artwork, and the lack of both helped to foster his sense of creative freedom. That's the kind of teaching and learning we'll be exploring here.

You've Got to Walk Before You Can Run

How did you learn to walk? You didn't take a class in it, read books, or take tests. You were much too young to read a manual and follow diagrams. You were even too young to watch somebody else do it and then consciously imitate them. You couldn't benefit much from having somebody coach you—although you probably had eager hands to guide you and to pick you up and comfort you when you fell.

But you learned to walk just the same, without anybody to teach you in any proper sense of the word. You didn't even need anyone to encourage or motivate you. Fact is, nobody could have stopped you if they tried.

Jeremiah began to walk before he was nine months old, a mixed blessing entailing a lot of parental pride and a lot of falling down. Ellen and I thought surely the hernia would slow him down, but it didn't. He was up and edging around the crib the day after the operation. He was ready to walk, and so he walked.

Learning to walk was surely one of the most complicated lessons of your life. How did you do it? I suppose you just kept trying until your body learned to make its minute adjustments, until you got "muscle smart," until your mind and body grew into the capacity to do what was in them to do all along.

Learning to Read, Planting a Seed and Other Miracles

Learning to read is like that. I taught kids how to read and adults how to read better for years. I know how to teach them to sound out words and to put the words together into sentences. But that isn't reading. Reading involves understanding the realities behind the words and interacting with those realities.

I've never been able to describe, predict or control that miracle. I don't know how it happens. One day a kid is still struggling to sound out "ma- ma- ma- MONKEY!" And the next day, face aglow with joy and astonishment, the kid is reading, really reading, and not just grunting out syllables.

Some kids get it pretty much on their own, without anybody really teaching them. Others never quite grasp it, no matter how much instruction and "remediation" (one of the ugliest words in the language) they receive. Some learn how to do it but never get the "why," the joy of it. For them it always remains work, a have-to and never a want-to. For me, reading is hobby, pleasure and daily necessity.

When I ran a reading lab at Solano Community College in California, I encountered a young man named Richard Handy who had somehow managed to wade through twelve grades of organized schooling while steadfastly remaining innocent of reading. But now Richard wanted to learn to read, and he was willing to put up with anything I saw fit to put him through to get the job done. I worked him hard, and his progress excited me. He never missed a lab session, he came in when the lab was open at lunchtime, and he came in between afternoon and evening classes to get in some more work.

Then he went home and read the dictionary. I mean that literally. He *read* the dictionary, starting with "aardvark" and plowing his way straight through. That's how much Richard Handy wanted to learn to read.

He later went on to law school.

I'm no more responsible for that miracle than the gardener is responsible for making the seed grow. We can plant and water, fertilize and weed, but we can't make the plant appear or explain how it accomplishes its miracle. Nor can we explain how one seed knows to be a stalk and ears of corn, another knows to be vines and pumpkins and a third to come up roses.

I can't explain how Richard Handy learned to read any more than I can explain how I did. I can't explain why some of the students in my labs never made much progress. "Motivation," you say. And I say, "Sure, motivation." But I can't explain where Richard Handy's intense motivation came from, and I can't explain why some of the other young men and women who passed through my lab lacked any hint or trace of it.

Learning Without Teaching

Try to recall a learning situation in which no one "taught" you, but you nevertheless learned. For me, learning to shoot a basketball falls into that category. I had very little instruction, none of it formal. I watched a lot of basketball on television, and then I went out onto the asphalt courts of Luther Burbank Elementary School and shot baskets — for hours, days, weeks, months and ultimately years.

I shot baskets in the rain and in the dark. I shot until my basketball got a bulge where the rubber wore too thin, and I had to beg my parents for a new basketball. I wore holes in my sneakers every three weeks from pivoting to shoot the hook shot. I shot free throws until I made ten in a row. Some days, that meant shooting hundreds of free throws.

I played full-court games by myself, Celtics against the Lakers,

Hawks against the Knicks, shooting the baseline jump shot like Bob Pettit or Dolph Schayes, the one-hand set shot like Bob Cousy, the jumper like Sam Jones, the free throw like Bill Sharman, the hook like Cliff Hagan. I kept box scores of each game in my head and wrote them down when I got home.

I did all this at a time in my life when my teachers would have described me as "unmotivated."

Nobody taught me, but I learned. And I never forgot. My fingers still know the feel of the basketball and the rightness of the shot.

Write a description of an instance of that kind of learning in your life. What motivated you? What was your reward? What did you learn about yourself in the process? In what sense can your writing be like that learning? How can you nurture your ability to grow into the writing that is within you to do?

In the course of remembering such a time of intuitive learning, you will come to trust yourself more fully to guide your own growth as a writer.

■■■■■■■■■■■■■■■■■

Exploration: Learning From the Mentor

 Remember a time when a mentor taught you skills and attitudes without actually instructing you in any formal sense. Write about that time, if you'd like, and reflect on what the experience can teach you about your writing. How do you feel about that mentor? Can you sense the presence of a loving, gentle mentor inside of you, waiting to guide you in ways beyond words?

Lessons of the Desert and the Forest

Your mentor can show you how to build a fire. But until you're camping in the desert or in the high mountains, temperature plunging with the setting sun, your fingers shaking with the new cold and your stomach growling for the food you must cook before you can eat, you don't really learn.

You must go from little to bigger to biggest, kindling to twigs to sticks. You must build air into your fire. You must give wood time to get hot enough before putting more wood on it. Your mentor can show you this, but then your mentor must let you build the fire for yourself. Only by building the fire will you learn to build the fire, and only by building the fire when you must have that fire to keep warm and to eat will you learn to build the fire when it counts.

Who can teach you how to sleep comfortably on hard ground? Your mentor shows you to dig hip holes in the desert sand and to gather pine branches in the forest. But when you go to sleep, your body figures out how often to roll and what position to assume. Who can teach it how to do that?

Who can teach your legs to find the survival pace on a hot day under a heavy pack on an endless trail?

Your mentor can tell you to suck pebbles to stave off thirst. But who teaches you how to endure the thirst when it comes despite the pebbles?

Your mentor can teach you the names of the trees and animals. But who teaches your heart to love them and to feel at ease among wild things? The heart is born knowing and must only be allowed to remember. The wise mentor allows the heart to remember.

George Cook was my mentor. He revealed all these things and many others to me, by bringing me to the desert and the forest and then trusting me to learn.

I saw my father take the pack from one who could carry it no further and put it onto his own back, along with his pack. What words could he have used to teach this lesson?

Learning From the Master Teacher

School is scary. Big strangers tell you what to do. Little strangers make fun of you. You're told to read or write or cipher and then you get laughed at if you do it wrong or if you do it right but not quickly enough and especially if you stammer and can't do it at all.

You get separated into groups. You're not supposed to know that your group is the dummies, but when your group is called the "magpies," and the other group is the "eagles," somehow you figure things out.

If you want very much to please and to earn praise, you do exactly what you perceive is expected of you. If you resent the pressure to please and to earn praise, you do exactly the opposite. You struggle to color between the lines, or you slash the page with wild scrawls. You stand quietly in line, or you make a run for it. Whichever way you respond, as a rebel or as a conformist, you risk losing any sense of what you would have done if not for the pressure to do something else.

Satirist H.L. Mencken recalled his school days with something less than unbridled affection.

> School-days, I believe, are the unhappiest in the whole span of human existence. They are full of dull, unintelligible tasks, new and unpleasant ordinances, brutal violations of common sense and common decency. It doesn't take a reasonably bright boy long to discover that most of what is rammed into him is nonsense, and that no one really cares very much whether he learns it or not.

Filmmaker Woody Allen is almost as acidic in his assessment of going to school.

> You'd go to school, where all was hostility and problems, even in the first grade. . . . The guys would be standing in line—there would be the fat kid that you hated in front of you, and the one with his nose running behind you, and these wretched little girls in the other line. And everybody would be standing there dreading that in a few minutes you'd march up to your class and go through hours of boredom and intimidation.

Student as Potted Plant

You often learned your lessons by rote, and then only long enough to recite correct answers on a test. It wasn't necessary that the stuff make sense or that it hook up to any experience in your life outside the school. You probably stopped expecting school to have much relevance to life very early on.

Honestly, now. How many times have you used the Pythagorean theorem? "Let's see now," you undoubtedly murmured as you tried to figure out how to replace the bedroom light fixture—the one that was overheating and threatening to burn your house down—"a square erected on the hypotenuse of a right triangle is equal to the sum of the squares erected on the other two sides."

How about balancing the valences on both sides of a chemical equation? That'll get the old checkbook squared away, right?

Unless you were very lucky, you learned math and science as an inert body of fact to be drilled into your head, instead of a dynamic group of guesses and discoveries, theories and confirmations, rejections and new theories, an evolution that you might be able to contribute to.

You were probably even force-fed literature as a series of facts to learn. Emily Dickinson became a code to crack and a test to pass instead of an experience to savor.

"Because I could not stop for _____, he kindly stopped for me."

1. the postman
2. lunch
3. death
4. a rest

The poems of Emily Dickinson may best be sung to the tune of:

1. "The Eyes of Texas Are Upon You"
2. "San Antonio Rose"
3. "The Yellow Rose of Texas"
4. "The Beer Barrel Polka"

Note: The correct answer to both questions is "3."

You probably had to memorize a teacher's opinions and recite them as fact. If your opinion didn't conform to the teacher's, and if you were foolish enough to write it down anyway, you received a bad grade.

Most adults, once having survived school, never read a book again. Not one. Is it any great mystery why? When we're treated this way, we may not learn much math, science or literature, but we learn the worst lesson school seems to want to teach us—that we're stupid, incurious and uncreative. What would we have learned if we hadn't been so busy being taught an awful lesson like that?

Failing to See the Forest for the Styrofoam Cups

As you got older, your learning probably became more self-directed, but you still may have gotten bogged down in externals (grades and credits) and structures (syllabus, curriculum, study guide). These things can become an end in themselves rather than the means to the end of learning.

Even when you're motivated to learn for its own sake, with no grades to worry about, you may get sidetracked. To learn to write, for example, you can take courses, read books, join critique groups, attend conferences and seminars, listen to self-help tapes. All of these can help you. None of them can teach you how to write.

In fact, sometimes the courses and critique groups can discourage you:

- By subjecting your immature, unfinished work to harsh judgment
- By comparing your infant work to the work of masters
- By increasing your self-consciousness as you write and thus destroying your ability to get out of the way and let the writing come
- By reinforcing your tendency to look outside of yourself for evaluations of your worthiness.

The learning and critiquing and discussing can take up all of your time and energy, leaving you nothing for the writing.

If the classes, workshops, groups and conferences do these things, they do you a great deal more harm than good.

We do learn good lessons, of course, sometimes despite our teachers, sometimes because a caring teacher gave us the precious gifts of trust and freedom. Here are a few examples of master teachers.

Giving Creativity Room to Grow

Stu Carlson calls it "living on the edge." Six days a week the *Milwaukee Sentinel* gives Carlson "that little rectangle to fill" on the editorial page, and six days a week, Carlson fills it with biting satire and cartoon commentary, usually aimed at Milwaukee politicians.

He works just one day ahead, with no backlog of ideas to rely on if he comes up empty.

"I have no idea of what I'm going to do," Carlson says, but he manages to produce a cartoon by 4:00 each afternoon to run in the following morning's paper.

"I need the deadline to make me do it," Carlson says.

Carlson got started cartooning early, drawing with lipstick on the walls of his parents' apartment. In school his teachers wrote home to ask his parents to "tell him to stop doodling in the margins."

One art teacher once gave him a "D."

"I think she didn't like me," Carlson says.

But a fourth-grade art teacher gave him a chance, letting him come in early or stay late to "do whatever you want to do." This master teacher gave Carlson more than just the run of the art room.

Carlson received trust and some room for his creativity to grow and develop.

More Portraits of Master Teachers

A while back, *USA Today* asked several prominent Americans, from a retired general to Public Television's Mr. Rogers, from government officials to baseball players, to describe a favorite teacher. They printed the results in a "Tribute to Teachers" spread.

Lou Brock, the baseball Hall of Famer, talked about accidentally hitting his third-grade teacher, Saphronia Young, with a spitball. For punishment, Young told Brock to go to the library and read about the history of baseball. What a punishment — to be allowed to explore a topic that already fascinated him. Brock learned, among other things, that baseball players got eight dollars a day in meal money. A career was born. And so was a friendship. "From then on," Brock wrote, "Miss Young and I were close."

Charles Kuralt, the CBS news reporter and wanderer of back roads, recalls "the only journalism teacher I ever had, or ever needed," Anne Batten. She told Kuralt to stop studying journalism and to study literature and history instead and to go to trials and City Council meetings to learn how government works. "Miss Batten made me believe journalism was important work, and that I could learn to do it," Kuralt wrote.

Carol Burnett remembers a sixth-grade teacher named Mrs. Ernst who used to read to the class and who threw herself so thoroughly into the reading that she "started crying real tears and screamed the way a real little kid would. . . . I think she was responsible for my choosing an acting career."

Giving Permission for Self-Respect

I've had several master teachers — and ex-Army sergeant named Krause, a one-legged journalism teacher named Clemens, a former political reporter named Rivers.

One of my master teachers came into my life when rheumatoid arthritis sent me to bed for six months and the school assigned me a home teacher to help me keep up with my schoolwork. After chatting with my mother in the living room, Mrs. Taylor would come into my room, her arms full of spellers and readers and math books, sit down beside my bed, and go over my lessons with me.

She didn't treat me like a cripple who needed special treatment.

She was there to work. She assumed that's what I was there for, too. I just happened to need to do my work flat on my back.

She didn't seem to know that I had been a rather poor student through most of the first six grades. She simply expected me to learn, and so I learned. She respected me, and by respecting me, she gave me permission to respect myself.

Stanley Sheinkopf's Crime and Punishment

When I was a senior in high school, another master teacher gave me that gift of respect. (That's the kind of gift we just can't get too often and never want to exchange for anything else, isn't it?) Mr. Sheinkopf was an immense, brooding man. His first name was Stanley, but I would no more have called him Stanley than I would have called the Pope "Paul" or "Johnny." Mr. Sheinkopf's scowl could quiet the most unruly class. He was a fiercely demanding teacher. I remember pacing the living room floor, going over and over my notes, over-studying for his world history exams.

One day just before Christmas vacation, he called me up to his desk after class. He smiled at me—he didn't do that much, and when he did, it seemed about as natural as a horse tap-dancing—and handed me a paperback copy of Dostoevsky's *Crime and Punishment*.

"I thought you might enjoy reading this," he said.

That was it—no explanation, no assignment, and no promise of extra credit. He just thought I might enjoy reading a huge novel full of small print and Russian names seventeen syllables long.

I did read it, every word of it. I struggled through the Russian names and the guilt and the philosophy. I'm not sure how much of it I understood, but I understood one thing quite clearly—Mr. Sheinkopf thought I could handle it. It wouldn't have occurred to me to try to read such a thing on my own, but Mr. Sheinkopf thought I not only could but that I'd like to, and I wasn't about to prove him wrong.

Forever after that, I was a man who could—and did—read Dostoevsky. If I could read Dostoevsky, I could read anything.

Somehow, with or without the help of a Mrs. Taylor or a Mr. Sheinkopf, we must claim our birthright as curious, creative individuals for whom learning is as natural as breathing. School can't teach us that, and it doesn't need to. School can—must—help us learn how to satisfy our curiosity and to express our creativity.

If school doesn't help us learn, if it teaches us instead that we are dim-witted and must be told all the answers, that we are not only unable but altogether unwilling to learn on our own and must be forced to the task, then we must learn our lessons elsewhere.

The master writer seeks out the teachers she needs. She finds whatever her writing must have to be complete. She reads, reflects, questions, grows. Nothing can stop her from learning. She learns, not because anyone expects her to or expects her not to or judges how well she does or doesn't do it, but because she must learn so that she can write, and she must write as well as she can to be truly, fully, herself.

■■■■■■■■■■■■■■■■■■■■■■■■
Exploration: Reexperiencing the Master Teacher

 Recall a teacher who nurtured you. Write a description of that teacher. Don't tell about her teaching. Show her in action. If you can't recall such a teacher, invent one.

What qualities in that nurturer helped you to learn and grow? Can you locate those qualities in yourself?

This exploration will help you to become your own master teacher, will help you to seek, find and understand whatever you need to know to create the writing that is within you to create.

Here's a reflection on a master teacher from my friend, master writer Betsy Anderson.

Remembering Mr. Bronson
I think it was because of his kind, compassionate and useful teaching that I survived high school.

As a nerd, I did what all other nerds did at my suburban Massachusetts high school—I took Latin. Mr. Bronson was our school's sole teacher of the dead language, but he was better known among the students for wearing seersucker suits and white shoes. He was a former Catholic priest who left the cloth to start a family.

Mr. Bronson had his own style of teaching Latin. The first day of class he said that Latin was not a dead language and therefore he was not going to teach it as such. During that first semester, we became his "Latin babies." He treated us as two-year-old Romans learning our native tongue rather than as twentieth-century Americans bored by the very idea.

Ubi est Roma? Roma in Italia est. Ubi sunt Roma et Graecia? Roma et Graecia in Europa sunt.

Second, third and fourth year Latin were taught in small tutorials. . . . As he sat with his big blue classics book squarely in front of him, he would bring to life the trials of the human condition described in those pages. He taught these literature passages to us much as a minister might preach to his flock from the Bible. . . . He used the pages of ancient Latin texts to describe the development of a person's character, emotions and role in society. Through Icarus and other now-forgotten myths and legends, I learned that there are challenges we all must face — with courage — if we are to be the people God wants us to be.

I remember tuning most of his God-stuff out, but it did plant a seed in my heart that only years later would I choose to cultivate.

Since the evening of graduation, I have never gone back to my high school nor tried to contact Mr. Bronson. He was old then (at least in a teenager's eyes) and he may have retired by now.

He may or may not remember me that clearly — if at all. But none of that really matters much. He was the teacher, I the pupil. Only in our case, it was not on academics that I needed lecturing, but in life. And skilled teachers of that course are rare indeed.

Imagine that your master teacher has been assigned to teach a class called *Creativity 101*. You are a student in that class. What is the class like? What do you do? How are you graded?

Here's my fantasy of a Creativity 101 course, taught by my master's degree advisor, master teacher Bill Rivers.

Creativity 101 à la Rivers
His grin is part Andy Rooney, part Mickey Rooney.

From his pack he takes out blossoms of quotes, bouquets of anecdotes, tufts and divots of hard data, and strews them on the table at the front of the class.

"Make a story," he says.

"What kind of story?" one of us—not I—asks. I was afraid to ask but hoped someone else would.

"We want a story the reader can get lost in," he says.

He steps back, his eyes on us. "Cast your net wide," he says.

We approach the table slowly, reach out to touch, draw back.

"They won't bite," he says.

He sits on a high stool and watches.

This isn't fair. He told us what to do, but he didn't tell us how.

"I'm not sure exactly what you want," the brave one among us says.

"Give your story whatever it needs," he replies.

We begin touching. We tentatively move things around. A pattern begins to emerge. He is beside us, prodding. "What happens if you do it this way?" he asks softly. And again, "Why did you put it there? What will that do for your story?"

Finally the story seems finished. We can think of nothing more to do.

"Is this right?" asks the one I had at first thought brave but now recognize as a coward like me.

Professor Rivers looks from us to the story. "Does it work?" he asks.

We look at what we have made.

"It's good," one says at last.

"Could be better," another says.

"What if we moved this quote up into the lead?" a third says.

"Yes," Professor Rivers says, nodding. "We'll try that tomorrow. Now it's time to go play volleyball."

The master learns the lessons that courses, books and seminars can teach her. Then she sets the not-writing aside and writes. As she writes, she lets her writing transform her, preparing her for the next writing. She focuses on the writing itself, and the writing flourishes in the intensity of that pure concentration. Even when she is not writing, her subconscious ponders and delivers its precious gifts of insight and awareness.

She learns whatever she must know to get the writing done well. Like a child teaching herself to walk, the master grows into an ability, an awareness and an insight that was in her all along.

13

Imagining

You owe reality nothing and the truth about
your feelings everything.
— *Richard Hugo*

"Write what you know."

If you've in any way made public your intention to be a writer, you've had this bit of wisdom thrust at you, probably many more times than once. And so you write about scrambling eggs and driving to work and falling in and out of love, because these are the things you know.

Imagine telling a child to "play what you know." What does a child know of rocket ships and rock stars, athletes and astronauts? And yet child's play is full of such things. What they don't know, they make up. And they do it with such élan.

"Wouldn't it be neat if this jungle gym were a rocket ship?" And so the jungle gym becomes a rocket ship and the child a rocket jockey.

It's so easy, so unself-conscious for the child. Is that why, when we approach a task with supreme confidence, we call it "child's play"?

Most of us grow cautious as we grow up. But inventors, pioneers and entrepreneurs retain that childish ability to play "let's pretend." They know that even the most grand and complex accomplishments all began as an infant idea.

A few of these dreamers also possess the skill and the persistence to make their imaginings become reality. Ed Janus has done it at least twice.

Bringing Baseball and Beer to Madison

Ed's first "wouldn't it be neat?" concerned bringing a minor league baseball team to Madison, Wisconsin. Madison had a team years ago, but local fans had learned to make the ninety-minute trek to Milwaukee's County Stadium to see major league ball (or at least an approximation of it), and some even go to Wrigley Field, Chicago to watch the Cubbies play.

A lot of folks told Ed minor league ball wouldn't work in Madison. But his dream—plus persistence, obstinacy, creative problem-solving and a lot of wrangling with the City Council—resulted in the awarding of a Class A franchise in Madison.

Ed defines creativity as "accident plus a damn good idea." He applied this formula to promoting the team, filling little Warner Park with raucous fans. The "Muskies" drew 120,000 their first season, a good mark for a Class A team. And those happy fans made national television with their antics. "I should pay to see them perform," the famous San Diego Chicken was heard to utter after appearing in the Fish Bowl.

The franchise just celebrated its tenth anniversary, but Ed has moved on, turning his energy, enthusiasm and ingenuity to another passion—German beer.

"Wouldn't it be neat?" he thought to himself one summer night, "if you could buy fresh beer that was as good as the imported stuff?" He went to the library and read up on brewing beer. He rented a building, hired a German brewmaster, and turned the combination into a brewery, making German-style beer in Madison.

Although both the baseball team and the brewery took massive amounts of work and worry—plus considerable risk of capital—they were projects of passion and thus "child's play" for Ed. They began with a simple vision in the mind of a man too impractical to realize that it couldn't be done.

"The Only Reason to Become a Journalist"

Erwin Knoll calls his position as editor of the *Progressive* magazine "the best job in America." Knoll works extremely hard at his job—writing, editing, lecturing, trying to keep a journal of political opinion and investigative reporting afloat in a society that doesn't tend to reward such endeavors. But he works out of a passionate desire to change the world, "the only reason to become a journalist," he says. And so the labor is joy-filled and fulfilling, and Knoll receives energy where others might become exhausted.

Knoll describes himself as "the only First Amendment absolutist" in America. He believes there should be no abridgments to freedom of the press—no libel or obscenity or privacy laws. Let the people speak, he says, and the truth will win out in the end.

Knoll's position was especially unpopular during America's participation in the Persian Gulf War, when the government placed severe restrictions on reporters' access to information. Knoll and a handful of other editors sued the government, calling its actions a violation of that First Amendment Knoll believes in so strongly and without reservation.

Agree with him or argue with him—and Knoll welcomes both responses—Knoll has dedicated his life to his vision. Because of the harmony this dedication produces in his life, all the hard work and contention are for Knoll child's play.

So it is for the master writer. To create her imaginings on paper, she must discipline herself and apply huge measures of time and energy. It's hard work. But for the master it's also play, not necessarily because it's fun (which it often isn't) but because the work is fueled by passion and by the fierce determination to make the project happen.

■■■■■■■■■■■■■■■■■■■■■■

Exploration: Remembering Your Child's Play

 Write about a time when the fun was all in the doing. How did you feel about your project—as you were doing it and after you had finished? What can that experience teach you about your writing?

My master-writer friend Cheri Nolan reflected on such an experience.

Building Forts

"Hey! Piedo, Fuddy, Chip. Let's build a fort." Easily done in the wide-open expanse that once was a thriving cherry orchard behind our house. The fun was in the building. The fort itself grew boring after a few days of escaping the world of adults.

Dragging empty appliance boxes home with our bike was only part of the challenge of fashioning a make-believe cardboard house.

Later, as an adult who babysat a myriad of children, I noticed the contentment the girls had in making and "living" in a multitude of ingenious tents in the living room.

Tents, forts, cardboard houses. Security, warmth, safety and temporarily a place of your own. One with your rules. Little havens from the pressure of growing up too fast.

Now think of a writing you'd like to do, regardless of any potential for publication or profit. Write a description of the project. Describe, too, how you might feel as you wrote it and after you finished.

What's to stop you from doing it? Write the first paragraph now. If you'd rather keep writing, set the book aside. We'll be here waiting when you're ready to read more.

Bag It or Bluff It

A fellow who calls himself "Dr. Science" comes on National Public Radio every now and again to answer listener questions. His made-up answers are wonderfully misinformative. Unlike most of the experts handing out advice through the media, Dr. Science knows he doesn't know what he's talking about.

You may have learned how to do a pretty good Dr. Science imitation in school. I know I did. I performed my act every time I got an essay question I couldn't answer on a test. I then faced the eternal choice: Bag it or bluff it. I could simply turn in an otherwise blank sheet of paper with my name on it, to show the teacher that I had at least shown up for class. Or I could put down everything I happened to remember that vaguely touched upon the topic at hand, and then go home and pray at the altar of the Great God of Partial Credit. In some courses, I lived on partial credit.

The most famous "bag it or bluff it" story I know concerns a student who hadn't studied his physics and faced a pop quiz in class. (Not studying promotes pop quizzes in exactly the same way that washing your car makes it rain.) The teacher scrawled this question on the chalkboard: "Using a barometer, how would you determine the height of the Empire State Building?"

Our unprepared student vaguely remembered hearing something about a formula having to do with altitude and barometric pressure. The higher you go, the lower the barometric pressure. If you got on the elevator on the ground floor of the Empire State Building, checked the pressure with your handy barometer, then rode to the top floor and checked the pressure again, you could plug the difference into a formula and figure out how high you had gone.

But the student didn't know the formula. Bag it or bluff it? He decided to bluff it. How about you? How many ways can you think of to figure out the height of a building using a barometer? Take a minute to play with ideas before reading on. Allow yourself to think silly thoughts.

Suction Cups and Shadows

I've given this problem to classes and workshops for years, and I almost always get an answer I'd never considered before. Here are a few of the best, ranging from fairly practical to downright far out (or up).

1. Measure the shadow cast by the building and the shadow cast by your barometer. Measure the height of the barometer. You now have three of the four elements of a simple ratio, which you can express as follows: the height of the barometer is to the length of its shadow as the height of the building (*X*) is to the length of its shadow. By cross-multiplying and then dividing, you'll get the height of the building (honest).

I don't know about you, but I'd heap partial credit on this answer, since it sounds a lot like physics and requires the use of some math.

2. Go to the top of the building with the barometer and a stop watch. (Notice that the question didn't say, "Using *only* a barometer. . . .") Drop the barometer over the side of the building and time its descent with the stop watch. (Notice, too, that the question didn't stipulate what shape the barometer had to be in when you were finished with it.) Using the formula for height and acceleration, you can compute the distance the barometer must have fallen (honest).

Mounds of partial credit for this one. It really *is* physics.

3. Again go to the top of the building, this time with the barometer, an exceedingly long rope, a piece of chalk and a tape measure. Tie the rope to the barometer and drop the barometer over the side of the building, paying out line until the barometer comes to rest on the sidewalk below. Mark the rope with chalk and haul the barome-

ter back up. Measure the rope from the barometer to the chalk mark and you'll have the height of the building.

Partial credit? At least you get your barometer back in working shape.

It gets worse (or better, depending on whether you want practicality or originality).

4. With your barometer and chalk and some super-strong suction cups for your hands and feet, scale the side of the Empire State Building, marking off lengths of the barometer as you go. Count the number of barometer lengths you marked off, multiply by the height of the barometer, and you'll have the height of the building.

5. Practical adaptation of #4: just measure one floor and then multiply by the total number of floors. Saves a lot of wear and tear.

Here's my all-time favorite:

6. Go to the basement and knock on the building superintendent's door. When he or she answers, say, "I'll give you this nice barometer if you'll tell me how tall this building is."

The teacher already knew how tall the Empire State Building is. If she didn't, she could look it up. (So could the students, for that matter.) She just wanted to find out if you had done your homework.

But in the real world, you really need the answer. Your way of finding that answer may be different than the textbook's way, but if you get the answer you need, your way is just as good. In fact, if your way is funny and inventive, it may be even better than the "right" way.

■■■■■■■■■■■■■■■■■■■■■■
Exploration: Bluff Writing

 Write a brief how-to essay about something you know nothing about. Don't research. Just imagine and use your intuition.

This exploration may bring back painful memories of some of those essay tests we talked about.

If you like, you can later research your topic and see how close you came to the correct procedures. Are your imaginings in any way better than the "right answers"? What does "better" mean in this case? Is it more fun to write when you aren't inhibited by the facts or under any obligation to be correct?

Here's my bluff-writing on a subject I know next to nothing

about, save what I've picked up from reading and watching Westerns.

Separating a Calf From the Herd for Branding

It's springtime, buckaroos, and time to get those bawling calves branded before the critters wander off and become mavericks—fair game for anybody with a branding iron, kindling and a match.

If you've got yourself a good, experienced cow pony, you've got half the battle won. Once he knows which calf you're after, that pony will do a lot of the work for you.

The first calf will be a little bit easier than the rest, because the calves won't have smelled fear and the hot iron yet. But your calf still isn't going to want to be parted from its mama. You're going to have a job of convincing on your hands.

Get yourself and your pony between the calf and its mama and then anticipate its every feint and dodge as it tries to get around you. Put your reins in your left hand and use pressure from your legs to direct your pony. Keep your hat in your right hand and whup it against your leg. The noise will keep the calf thinking about you instead of about mama.

Work the calf away from its mama and to the outside of the herd. Work with the sun over your shoulder if you can, to prevent the calf from getting a good, clear look at where it's been and where it would rather be again.

That calf will be setting up a real tizzy-fit by now. She's scared, and you've just taken her away from food, protection and that warm, wet tongue of love. Keep her moving, so there's no time for introspection.

Cows ain't the smartest of God's critters. The rest of the herd will be highly sympathetic to the calf's plight, but it won't occur to them that there's hundreds of them and only just the one sore-legged, dusty-eyed saddle tramp taking their buddy from them. They won't start any revolutions.

Now that you've got clear ground between you and the branding fire, get your rope off the saddle horn and slide the noose over the calf's head. (It ain't like the movies, where they sling the rope from three counties away, but then again, cowboys don't really mount their horses by jumping off of hotel balconies, either.)

Loop your end of the rope twice around the saddle horn, slide off your horse on the side away from the calf, so as not to get tangled in the rope, drop your reins (your pony's signal to hold its ground) and run to the calf. Toss 'er quick and lash back and front legs together with your hand rope.

There just isn't anything quite like a kicking calf, so there isn't anything to practice this move on except a kicking calf. You'll get quicker with practice.

Find the smoothest surface on the flank you can. Make sure the branding iron's hot enough. Some say it doesn't hurt the calf none, but I've never heard a calf say so. Make it quick. Notch the ear while you've got 'er down, as neither one of you is gonna want to go through this again any time real soon. Untie and jump clear, to the side away from the herd. She'll forget about you and take off for her mama and some cow consolation.

Next lesson: castration made easy.

If you know how this procedure is really done and would like to set me straight, feel free to write to me in care of the publisher. But know that I've already had my fun and like my version quite well, thank you.

■ ■

Exploration: Applying Bluff Writing to Writing Fact

 This kind of exploration can serve you well when you need to be accurate and have amassed a great deal of research on your subject.

You could dive right into your notes, cutting and pasting, trying to shape all the pieces into a coherent whole. But often this method yields a choppy, halting piece of writing rather than the smooth read you're after.

Instead, try a variation on the bluff-writing technique. Read over your notes two or three times, making marginal comments and underscoring key elements. Set the whole mess aside and let it simmer for a bit, perhaps even overnight, so that your subconscious can have a crack at it. You'll be making the material your own, hooking it to other information and to your experience.

When you're ready to write, set your notes aside. If you feel that it would be helpful, sketch a quick outline of the key points you'd like to make. But keep it simple, like the pencil sketches an artist makes before beginning a painting. Then write the whole piece without looking back at your notes.

Write with as much assurance—bluff—as you can, even if you're not sure you've got the information straight. If you confront a gap in your knowledge, skip a few lines and continue with what you do know. Strive for smoothness, and strive, too, to capture whatever excitement the subject warrants. Be loose and conversational. Use metaphor and imagery whenever you can.

Set your writing aside, to let it cool and to give your subconscious one more crack at it. Then revise and rewrite carefully, using your notes to make necessary corrections and to fill in the blanks. Go back a second time to trim the fat and rein in the excess. Then go back one more time, imagining yourself to be the reader confronting the piece. Ask, "What's in it for my reader? Why would anyone want to read this?" Make sure you've answered reader questions and anticipated reader needs.

You're likely to have that smooth, interesting read that you wanted, with no seams showing.

■ ■
Exploration: Describing Place

 Now let's apply the bluff-writing technique to a description of place. Select a place you know well, a place with possibilities. If the prospect of writing about your basement excites you, go for it, but it might be more fun to tackle something a bit more exotic. You might want to recall a place you haven't seen in a while.

I have stored vivid memories of many places I've lived and visited. I didn't know I was doing so at the time, but store them

I did, in just the way Helen Hooven Santmyer describes in her lovely *Ohio Town: A Portrait of Xenia.*

> If the skies were clear, you almost certainly paused at the gate, with a hand on the latch, to search for the first star in the west, to wish for escape and a brilliant future far, far away — and yet at the same instant you were aware of the iron of the gate beneath your hand, and were storing away the memory of how it felt. Thus the unfastidious heart makes up its magpie hoard, heedless of the protesting intelligence.

Here's a description of one of the places I stored while growing up.

Columbine Lake, Colorado

Did we go there just two summers? And yet I remember it so well, and I've gone back to it in my mind so many times — a lake small enough to walk around, large enough to make it a hike, isolated enough to make the hike an adventure.

I see the sun setting across the lake, silhouetting the pines. I'm on the porch of our cabin. Dad is down by the shore, fishing. I'm sure there are jays and squirrels chattering, but I remember the moment in stillness.

The cabin has one main room of kitchen, breakfast booth and bedroom-alcove with a curtain for privacy. There is a bedroom off the kitchen and a bathroom across from the alcove. A large window gives onto the porch and the lake beyond.

We walk down the dirt road to the lodge and the small, sandy beach. The sand is wet from the brief rain shower that comes every afternoon. The lake water is cold enough to command attention and to ring my neck with sharp pain when I dive in. But after a few moments of frantic exertion, the lake becomes an embrace, and I float, watching the sky until I feel myself becoming a part of it.

Sometimes we took the road for perhaps another mile beyond the lodge to the county road that goes into town, Grand Lake, nothing grand about it, but a movie house, miniature golf, grocery, all that we need.

Applying Bluff to Travel Writing

I've used bits of Columbine Lake in my fiction, those silhouetted trees and the feeling of stillness, and I know I'll go back again to help me create a sense of place.

If I wrote an article about this little jewel for a Sunday newspaper travel section, I would, of course, have to gather facts, assemble mileage charts, list nearby attractions and points of interest. I might even get into the history of the area, if it proved to be interesting. But I would begin with the feel of the Lake and my memories of it. Perhaps none of my bluff-writing would appear in the finished piece, but it would center and focus me for the task and would remind me of the reason for writing at all.

■ ■ ■ ■ ■ ■ ■ ■ ■ ■ ■ ■ ■ ■ ■ ■ ■ ■

Exploration: Creating Fictional Place

 Now all that remains is the ultimate bluff, to write convincingly, lovingly, in rich, textured detail, about a place that doesn't exist anywhere but in your imagination. Using the "notes" you've been gathering in your "magpie hoard" all of your life, everywhere you've ever been, you can build a convincing fantasy, the kind of fictional lie that somehow achieves an emotional truth in the reader.

"Before we made fire," Wright Morris wrote, "before we made tools, we made images. . . . That is what we were, and this is still what we are."

Take a few minutes right now to describe a place that exists only in your mind.

I open my novel, *The Year of the Buffalo*, with a description of the town I've created for my characters to live in. I see some of my hometown of Altadena, California, here, some of Miles City, Montana, a dab of Mexico, Missouri, some of Wausau, Waterloo, and Mineral Point, Wisconsin, and bits of a few towns I've visited only in the fiction of other liars.

Coming Back to Beymer

Dutch crossed the bridge spanning the narrow Oshnaube River and stopped to take in the three blocks of Main Street, Beymer, Wisconsin.

There wasn't much to take in.

The street was late Sunday afternoon deserted. American flags hung limply from the street lamps. The one signal light went stolidly through its cycle—red, blinking yellow, yellow, green. All the scene needed, Dutch thought, was a sleeping dog in the middle of the street. But it was too cold for dogs to be sleeping in streets.

Dutch had walked to his boarding house from the bus station, stayed long enough to drop his bags and meet his landlady—a short, Scandinavian widow who acted as if Dutch smelled bad, which he undoubtedly did—and set off for downtown. He told himself he was looking to find food. But now that he had found what the landlady—Hughes, Hagen, Haugen—had referred to as the "bidness district," he decided maybe it was just the walk he had wanted, because it looked as if it was just the walk he was going to get.

The sun, still about thirty degrees off the horizon, lined up with the end of the street, so that it was right in his eyes as Dutch descended the slight slope into town. He wondered if that were some sort of omen.

The building facades were made of the same stone blocks as the bridge he had just crossed and, like the blocks of the bridge, were cracked and crumbling. Either they had worn a lot in the thirty-five years since Dutch had seen them, or he hadn't noticed how worn they had been the first time around.

He passed Salibee's Five and Dime, which had a ragged yellow ribbon tied to the door handle and a hand-lettered sign in the window admonishing passersby to "Support our Troops in Heida," Tilbury's Toggery and another yellow ribbon, an empty store front that still had a sign in the window announcing the Valentine's Day dance at the Town Hall, Lenny's Appliance—sales and service and three yellow ribbons, another empty store front, The Hotel Beymer, The Buffalo Club, with inevitable martini glass with olive, Neuhauser's Pharmacy, with a sign under the clock that read, "We have the time/to serve you." The clock showed 6:27. A yellow ribbon tucked up under the clock like a bib.

Dutch stopped and looked in at the "Dime a Cup Cafe."

"Free pie and coffee for our service men and women," a hand-scrawled sign in the window announced. Inside, a woman stood behind the counter. She looked to Dutch to be about thirty-five and not trying to look any younger. She had that look of waitresses in small-town diners — damp bangs matted on her forehead, mouth turned down, eyes tired. Too many meatloaf specials served, too many refills poured, too many bad jokes and lame passes fended off.

As Dutch watched, she shifted her weight from her left to her right leg, and her left hip, the one closest to the window, thrust out toward Dutch. The movement stirred something in him.

She had the inevitable coffeepot in her hand and, as Dutch watched, she leaned over the counter and poured for a fat old man in coveralls and seed cap. Dutch had seen him before, too, in every diner at every hour in every town he'd ever passed through.

The old man said something, and the woman laughed. As she did, the age lifted from her face, and her eyes seemed young with the laughter. She really didn't look like all those other waitresses after all, Dutch decided. There was something about her expression, not defiance, exactly, but something like defiance and more than mere endurance.

She knows who she is, Dutch decided.

14

Surrendering

The greater the author, the less he understands his own work.
— C.S. Lewis

Kids don't have any power. We're always telling them what to do and when to do it. Adults call childhood "carefree," but from the kid's point of view, it's "control-free." Life for a child is a lot about surrendering. Much of growing up is a battle to gain control — over parents, over peers, over emotions, over life.

But if kids don't have much freedom, they don't have many responsibilities, either. They're innocent of consequences, and they don't know they have anything to lose.

The older we get, and the more possessions and responsibilities we accumulate, the bigger the consequences of every decision, whether we make them for ourselves or somebody makes them for us. As we struggle to carry our growing burden, we may fool ourselves into thinking we're in charge, not only of paying bills and getting to work on time, but of our inner gift of creativity. Like the rooster that believes that his crowing brings up the sun each morning, we may try to take credit for our inspirations and blame ourselves for our blocks and banalities.

We may fail to accept inspiration as gift, twisting in on ourselves instead to try to discover how we created and worrying that we may never be able to create again. Energy turns to frustration, which turns to stress, which translates into headaches, ulcers, chronic sleeplessness and other physical symptoms and in alcohol and drug abuse and other attempts at self-medicating our pain.

Can you turn all your stress and anxiety back into pure energy when you write? Could you use all of your hard-won wisdom and life-learning while still tapping your childish gusto? You can if you attempt to take no credit for your gift and no blame for the limitations of that gift. Focus not on the writer but on the writing. This is another way of saying that you must get out of the way, must lose yourself in your writing.

Taking Responsibility for What You Write

But conversely, you must take total responsibility for stewardship of your gift. Will you allow it to flourish and grow? Or through neglect and abuse, will you cause it to wither and perish?

Whether you write well or poorly, whether you publish or hide your manuscript under a bushel, whether you write at all or engage in various forms of not writing, you must take total responsibility, must own your actions. Your eleventh-grade English teacher didn't make you not write. It's not your mother's fault. Don't blame that editor in New York who told you that you had no talent. It's just you and the keyboard or the pad of paper. You're responsible for what happens next.

With that responsibility comes a kind of control. You get to decide what, when and where you'll write. With control comes energy and even exhilaration. It may feel a lot like anxiety at first, especially if you're not used to it. But this is good stress, the thrill the skydiver feels at the moment of freedom from the airplane.

Take the lid off. Let it rip. It's all yours. When you write, you're in charge.

And then you must hand over your control to the inspired voice inside you and allow it to create.

Uncaging the Dream Beast

As adults, we prize self-control. We say of the person who remains calm in an emergency, "She's really got it together." We may like passionate surrendering in the fiction we choose to read, but we are usually much more cautious in our own dealings.

When we try to suppress our impulses and emotions, we may create what Freud called "the beast in the basement" and Jung labeled "The Shadow."

"We fear to know the fearsome and unsavory aspects of our-selves," psychologist Abraham Maslow wrote.

The feelings don't go away; they go underground, to surface in our dreams. Who is that, having the wild, erotic sexual fantasy or the vivid, terrifying nightmare? Surely not *you*? Yes, you. But in dreams you are out of your conscious, controlling mind.

Psychologist Mary Edwards says that such surrender into dreaming is good and necessary. Even your most terrifying night-mares are a part of a benevolent process, she says, bringing you to your "edge of change," so that you may take the next tentative steps on your journey.

The master knows this childlike sense of surrender in waking life. She gives herself up to her creation. Rather than trying to take control of her writing, she lets it take control of her. She becomes the instrument, and the creation occurs through her.

The master must lose herself to gain her writing, must in a sense die to live, must go out of her mind to draw on the larger mind— call it "Big Mind," if you will—outside the narrow bands of her conscious "Little Mind."

Getting the Guilt out of the Ice Cream

Kids'll eat too much ice cream if you let them. *Way* too much ice cream.

Adults will eat too much ice cream, too, but they'll hear the meter running, counting all those calories. You can feel the fat forming on the hips even as the ice cream slides over the lips.

You eat it, but you feel guilty about it, and often the guilt sours the ice cream. You wind up with all the calories but none of the enjoyment.

Maybe it won't be quite as bad for you if you eat it in small bites, right? Or if you only eat it after you've eaten your lima beans. Or if you promise yourself you'll skip breakfast tomorrow. That's certainly not how a kid eats ice cream. A kid will shovel it in—before or instead of the lima beans—if we let her. Making deals takes some of the fun out of eating ice cream, especially when the taste of those limas lingers.

We, of course, have to learn to curb our appetites or pay heavy penalties for overindulgence. But in the process of learning to re-strain ourselves, we risk forgetting how to enjoy the food we eat, the water we drink, the sweet morning air that is the very breath of life.

Breathe deeply. Partake fully of the exhilarating gift of life and of the birthright of creativity that comes with it. If you choose to eat the ice cream, surrender to the ice cream. Enjoy every atom of the sweetness.

If you choose to spend your time writing—whether you look on writing as ice cream or lima beans—surrender completely to the writing. Be wholly present to the experience. Lose yourself into the writing, without giving a thought to whether or not you should be doing it. You've already made that decision.

Perhaps you choose not to eat the ice cream. You may feel noble and angry and resentful, while those around you are loudly enjoying their ice cream, and the ice cream you didn't eat seems infinitely sweet.

Enjoy, too, the rightness of the denial when you decide not to eat the ice cream. Savor the emptiness, the taste the ice cream isn't making in your mouth because you chose not to let it. Without lording it over your friends ("Do you have *any* idea how many calories are in that thing?"), affirm your decision and get on with whatever's next.

So, too, for those times when you choose to do something other than writing. When you've made your decision, give yourself wholly to the not-writing, without letting guilt or regret nag at you. (They will try. When they do, gently, firmly talk back to them and send them away.) That way, you'll do whatever you're doing well, and when you return to your writing (which, after all, will surely wait for you), you'll be clear, refreshed and focused.

Learning to Accept the Gift

Picture the family gathered around the tree on Christmas morning. All the preparation, all the anticipation, all the agony of waiting is at an end. It's time for the opening of the gifts.

Mom opens her package with maddening care. First she removes the ribbon and sets it aside to use another day. She's careful not to rip the paper and smooths it out for saving. When the blouse is finally released from its bondage, she oohs and aahs, examines the treasure from every angle, assures the giver that it is exactly and precisely what she wanted and needed and, in fact, couldn't have possibly lived another minute without. Then she must try it on before the unwrapping can go any further.

All this is driving the kids nuts, of course.

Finally, Mom returns in the new blouse, receives her compliments, and Dad picks out one of his presents. He shakes the box, holds it to his ear and begins to speculate on its contents.

"I don't hear any ticking," he says. "I guess it's not a bomb."

Now Junior's really going bonkers.

Dad finally liberates his tie or socks or copy of *Angling Made Easy*. It's Junior's turn at last.

A carnage of ripping and tearing, an orgy of gift-lust. The toy lays exposed in seconds.

Kids accept gifts with great gusto. A kid will never say, "Oh, you shouldn't have" or otherwise question the motives of the giver or the worthiness of the recipient. Of *course* you should have, and please do it again.

The master writer accepts the gift of inspiration with similar enthusiasm. These gifts come from the larger mind that surrounds and informs consciousness. She doesn't question her worth or the worth of the inspiration. She embraces.

En Theos: "God Within"

I've already told you about Rod Sherman, Mr. Everything from John Muir High School Class of '62, but I haven't told you about his laugh.

Rod's laughter used to fill the halls and spill out into the pergola and the playing fields. His laugh could knock down doors, including the doors of other people's reserve. You couldn't not join in. It was the happiest, most uninhibited laugh I've ever heard—infectious, raucous, unruly. In short, Rod Sherman—star quarterback, class president and general all-around superhero—laughed like a little kid.

Adults don't laugh that way. Often, the laughter of an adult (if they laugh at all) is forced and tentative, little better than a strangled burp that dies in the throat. Some of us cover our mouths when we laugh, as if embarrassed. What if my laughter is inappropriate? What if it offends? What if what I'm laughing at isn't really funny? (Says who?)

The master may not find anything funny about writing. One writer friend of mine, Winifred Wise, likes to say that writing is "about as much fun as having an elephant step on your foot." She has published eighteen books, so she must enjoy having the pachyderm trample her tootsies at least a little bit, but she makes a good point.

The master brings a fierceness, an energy, an enthusiasm to the encounter, fun or not, and it shows in the writing. That's no small matter. "Enthusiasm" comes from the Greek "en" for "within" and "theos" for "God." To be enthused, then, is to possess an inner spark of the divine.

Drift, Wait and Obey

Rudyard Kipling called this inner voice his "Personal Daemon."

"Mine came to me early when I sat bewildered among other notions, and said, 'Take this and no other,'" Kipling wrote in *Something of Myself.* "I obeyed, and was rewarded."

Kipling learned to rely on this inspiration. "My Daemon was with me in the Jungle books, Kim and both Puck books, and good care I took to walk delicately, lest he should withdraw," Kipling wrote.

"When your Daemon is in charge," he concluded, "do not try to think consciously. Drift, wait, and obey."

Henry Wadsworth Longfellow had a similar experience of drifting into inspiration. The tale is recounted in *The Life of H.W. Longfellow.*

> Last evening, I sat till twelve o'clock by the fire, smoking, when suddenly it came into my mind to write the "Ballad of the Schooner Hesperus," which I accordingly did. Then I went to bed but could not sleep. New thoughts were running in my mind, and I got up to add them to the ballad.... It did not come into my mind by lines but by whole huge stanzas.

Contemporary novelist Zev Chafets described his inspiration in more modern terms in the *New York Times Review of Books*:

> In the first few weeks that I was writing the book [*Inherit the Mob*], it was like watching a movie in my head. I sort of wrote down what I saw. Every day that I got up from the computer, I was afraid that the movie wouldn't come back the next day.

Entirely Alone, and of Good Cheer

Such gifts aren't limited to writers. Composers get them, too. Here's Wolfgang Amadeus Mozart, writing to a friend:

> When I am, as it were, completely myself, entirely alone, and of good cheer—say, traveling in a carriage or walking after a

good meal, or during the night when I cannot sleep; it is on such occasions that my ideas flow best and most abundantly. Whence and how they come, I know not; nor can I force them. . . . Nor do I hear in my imagination the parts successively, but I hear them, as it were, all at once. What a delight this is I cannot tell! All this inventing, this producing, takes place in a pleasing lively dream.

The process isn't always so placid. Tchaikovsky wrote that his compositions came "suddenly and unexpectedly . . . with extraordinary force and rapidity. . . . I forget everything and behave like a madman; everything within me starts pulsing and quivering."

He Is Now to Be Among You . . .

Check the album notes for the haunting, beautiful "Wedding Song," which has probably been performed at more weddings than any other song in creation, and they'll tell you that Noel Paul Stookey (the "Paul" in "Peter, Paul and Mary") wrote the words and music.

But Stookey doesn't tell it that way. He says the song wrote him.

In my last book, *Freeing Your Creativity: A Writer's Guide*, I told part of the story of how Stookey came to write that song. I later wrote and asked Stookey for the rest of the story, and he generously wrote back and gave it to me. It's a marvelous illustration of the literal meaning of "en Theos."

Peter Yarrow (another third of that great folk trio) asked Stookey to write a song to bless his upcoming marriage to Mary Beth McCarthy. Stookey took the request seriously and literally. "Knowing that the blessing would have to come from God," Stookey wrote, "my responsibility was to find some musical means to do that."

A week or so later, by Stookey's own account, he was sitting in his studio, paper, pencil and guitar at the ready. He waited and prayed. "And the words came," Stookey wrote: " 'I am now to be among you at the calling of your hearts.' . . . The song came first person, just that way."

An hour before the wedding, Stookey played the song for his wife, Betty, who advised him to change it from first to third person, so that people would understand the message more clearly.

"Every aspect of the song was perfect for that particular moment," Stookey wrote. Later, when Yarrow requested that Stookey perform the song at a concert, Stookey gave his beautiful blessing to anyone who wished to accept it.

The Seventeen-Year Flash of Inspiration

Scientific breakthroughs really aren't that different from artistic ones. "At the highest levels of thought," psychologist Frank Farley says, "art and science may be the same." Scientists get the pulsing and quivering of inspiration, too, as evidenced by the astounding story of Otto Loewi, winner of the 1936 Nobel Prize in physiology. Loewi discovered and demonstrated that the nerve impulses that are the basic component of all nervous systems are both chemical and electrical in nature, a major breakthrough that is helping us now to understand the relationship between brain, mind and body.

Early in his career, Loewi had a hunch, a wild idea. But he couldn't think of any way to test it. It was just a fleeting tease, one of the hundreds any good scientist, artist, mathematician or master writer gets.

Seventeen years later, the idea came back, this time in a dream. Loewi wrote about it in an autobiographical sketch:

> The night before Easter Sunday of the year 1920 I awoke, turned on the light, and jotted down a few notes on a tiny slip of paper. Then I fell asleep again. It occurred to me at six o'clock in the morning that during the night I had written down something important, but I was unable to decipher the scrawl. The next night, at three o'clock, the idea returned. It was the design for an experiment to determine whether or not the hypothesis of chemical transmission that I had uttered seventeen years ago was correct. I got up immediately, went to the laboratory, and performed a simple experiment on a frog's heart according to the nocturnal design. . . . Its result became the foundation of the theory of chemical transmission for the nervous system.

■ ■
Exploration: Flow-Writing

 What does feeling "inspired" mean for you? Do you become seized with an urge to write? Do you receive an image, a clear picture of what you want or need to write about? Is the image in black and white or color? Soft pastels or bright primaries?

Does the inspiration come in the form of a word, a phrase, perhaps a line or two? Is it loud, like a tornado, or soft, the still, small voice in the breeze?

Do you recognize it when it comes? If you expect a tornado, you might not hear that smaller, calmer voice. If you're looking for words, you might miss the picture. Inspiration can come in many guises, with many voices or with no voice at all.

What do you do with inspiration when you receive it? You can ignore, discount, even belittle your inspiration. (*If I thought of it, it can't be worth that much.*) Do that enough times, and you'll stop having any inspirations.

Or you can pounce upon the infant inspiration so hard, you crush it before it can grow. You can try to make a phrase be a whole poem, try to turn an image into a five-hundred-page novel.

Next time you receive an inspiration, be it specific words or images or simply the urge to write, pick up pencil or pen and notebook and write whatever wants to come out. Let the inspiration unfold without trying to shape or refine, trim or expand it. Don't tell it where to go. Let it lead you to someplace you haven't been before.

Keep writing until the inspiration seems to have passed. Then sit quietly, pencil and notebook close at hand, and wait to see if more wants to come. Set the writing aside, letting your larger mind continue to play with, layer and refine your idea.

When you go back and read what you've written, you'll find surprises. You may also find that Big Mind is now ready to add more.

Become accustomed to doing this kind of flow-writing often. If you pay this sort of attention to your inspirations, you will begin having more and more of them to pay attention to.

■ ■ ■ ■ ■ ■ ■ ■ ■ ■ ■ ■ ■ ■ ■ ■ ■

Exploration: Directed Flow-Writing

 Learn, also, to create inspiration when you need it. Sit with that pencil or pen and notebook. Indicate at the top of the page the subject you wish to write about. It may be a part of the writing project you're currently working with, or it may be a word or phrase that has meaning for you.

To prepare yourself for these encounters, you might want to brainstorm a list of such words and phrases. Here are a few examples that have significance for me:

- The house I grew up in
- Fishing with my father
- Little League baseball/stew for dinner
- Climbing to the top of the pine tree on LaPaz Road
- Camping alone on Henniger Flats
- Two-year-olds braving day-care for the first time
- A dog's cold nose and warm heart

Using your word or phrase as point of departure, begin writing freely. Write whatever comes to mind. Again, don't try to shape or force it. Let it go where it pleases. If you find yourself straying too far from your original departure point, you may choose to explore the new tangent if it appears to be more interesting than the road you had intended to travel, or you may gently nudge yourself back to your subject.

Since you don't have a specific destination in mind, you can't ever be lost. Let your mind roam.

Do a directed flow-writing whenever you're stuck. You can write yourself out of most any "writer's block" you'll ever create.

Get in the habit of doing this sort of directed flow several times a month, stuck or not. Save these writings in your notebooks and go back to them from time to time. You'll find wonderful ideas, images and phrases. You'll also encounter a self you weren't consciously aware of, a creative and inventive self you'll want to draw on often in your writing.

15

Creating Collisions

Whatever you can do, or dream you can, begin it. Boldness
has genius, power and magic to it.
— Goethe

Most kids aren't very good at waiting. Try to make one sit still, and
right away the foot starts jiggling. Soon the leg catches the fever,
and before long the whole body has a serious case of the squirms.
For kids, waiting is agony. They've got to be up and doing.

Putting a baseball game in front of that wriggling kid may not
help much. You can buy a bit of peace with hot dogs and peanuts,
but when the stomach can hold no more, the body again wants to
be in motion. Kids are better at doing than watching.

Television may be changing all that. Kids now spend as much
time staring at the tube as they do sitting in the classroom. We're
probably making a rather large mistake here, sedating the kids when
we should be activating the adults.

A lot of adults aren't much good at waiting, either. Study the
faces of drivers trapped in rush hour gridlock, and you'll witness an
abstract portrait of impatience. But when it comes to creative effort,
some grown-ups have lost the energy and headlong drive of the
children they were and have chosen instead to wait.

What Are You Waiting For?

John P. Robinson, a professor of psychology at the University of
Maryland, has spent the last twenty-five years of his time studying
how his fellow Americans use theirs. Despite all testimony to the

contrary, Robinson says he has charted a steady increase in the amount of free time we have. "The perception of a time crunch appears to have gone up in the period of time when free time has increased," Robinson says.

According to the professor's research, since 1965, men have gained seven hours of free time per week (from thirty-four to forty-one hours), and women have gained six (thirty-four to forty). And all of it has gone into watching television. The tube eats up almost 40 percent of our nonwork, nonchore, nonsleep time, Robinson reports.

We use lack of time as an excuse to avoid doing what we don't want to do, Robinson says, while we make time for what we do want to do.

When Robinson began his research, he expected to find that some folks attend a lot of cultural events, for example, while others stay home and fix their carburetors. But he found that some folks do both — a lot of concert going and a lot of tinkering — while other folks don't seem to do much of anything. Robinson's research verifies the adage, "To get a thing done, find a busy person," and the old 80/20 rule that states that 20 percent of the people accomplish 80 percent of the work. "The more you do one thing," Robinson concludes, "the more you do another." He applies Newton's Law to people's activity levels: "Bodies in motion tend to stay in motion."

We used to call such perpetual-motion personalities "Type-As." Robinson calls them "omnivores." Instead of trying to "cure" them with meditation tapes, tranquilizers or mantras, he readily admits to being one of them and embraces the whole notion of staying active.

We can learn from Robinson — and from all those squirming, jiggling children. We'll never get anywhere if we don't get moving. You want to have written? Then start writing.

Type-T People and Creativity

"If you can't explain your theory to your barkeep, it stands no chance," Frank Farley says.

Farley is a psychology professor at the University of Wisconsin-Madison. Lately, he's been explaining his theory of the Type-T personality on network morning news shows and in the pages of *Cosmopolitan*, *New Woman*, *USA Today* and other popular publications.

"Knowledge should be out on the street, changing the world," Farley says. "Most professors are talking to their navels."

Here's how Farley might explain his theory to his barkeep:

Some people are much more likely to seek out risk. These are the Type-Ts (for thrill-seekers). At the other end of the spectrum, little-t types seek certainty and stability.

"At the juncture of all great progress, you'll find a T-type," Farley says. "How do you change? How do you grow? You take a risk. . . . Creative people are much more open to ideas."

Farley's openness to ideas led him to attempt to communicate with the dead and record the results. When the tape stubbornly remained blank, Farley concluded, "I don't think the other side speaks."

But he remains open to possibilities. "The one thing I've learned . . . is not to be close-minded," he says. "The history of science is the total overturning of ideas."

The TV Generation Goes to School

"The book is on the wane," Farley warns. Today's kids are products of the television era, and "it's getting harder and harder to handle these kids in the classroom using traditional means."

We've viewed kids as passive "receptacles of knowledge," he says. "We'd cram the stuff in and they'd regurgitate it." But we now know that the mind is active, Farley notes, that it in fact constructs and reconstructs the input it receives and that it edits reality constantly.

"Thirty kids in a classroom will construct thirty realities," he says.

Fact is, so will thirty adults.

How about you? How are you educating that curious child inside you? Are you treating yourself as a passive receptor rather than an active learner?

Specifically, are you spending more of your time watching television these days rather than reading books, magazines and newspapers? Television may be a more passive means of experiencing life and gaining information, but only if you let it be. You can absorb television in a passive way, letting it wash over you like a lukewarm shower. You can view uncritically and unselectively, choosing to watch television rather than choosing to watch a particular show.

Or you can choose selectively and engage television actively, processing information, questioning it, relating it to other information, testing your theories about life, and affirming, modifying or discarding those theories.

In that way, television can help to supply you with the raw materials of experience and information you must have to create.

But you must also have the strength to get up, turn off the television, and set yourself to the task of creating.

What Makes Us Creative?

Psychologist Carl Rogers lists three inner conditions necessary for creativity to flourish. (He lists two outer conditions, too, which we'll get to in a bit.)

First, the creative individual must be *open to experience*. That means being attentive and taking it all in, but it also means accepting experience for what it is. The creative individual has a tolerance for ambiguity and chaos. She doesn't try to force meaning or closure onto a situation. She accepts failure and disintegration as a prelude to breakthrough and integration into a new, better order.

Second, the creative personality *evaluates the value of her creative effort for herself* and not by the praise or criticism of others. She isn't closed to feedback, but she reserves final judgment for herself.

And finally, the creative individual *plays with ideas, images and words*. From this play comes the hunch, and from the hunch comes the new vision.

That's Rogers's way of looking at it. Here's my way of describing the same phenomenon.

The Type-C Theory of Creativity

Creative people (Type-Cs) have lots of collisions. Notions fly around in the mind of the Type-C like Ping-Pong balls in a wind tunnel. The movement is random, and the notions run into each other a lot. The collisions throw off sparks, which occasionally ignite into flames of inspiration. Or ideas couple, creating new ideas.

Most of the inspirations and couplings are useless, silly or downright unmentionable. A few are original and apt. And occasionally, randomly, usually without warning, the Type-C gets the kind of brainstorm that shakes the world.

But somebody who has never picked up a guitar doesn't suddenly write a "Wedding Song." Paul Stookey, who has become a master of music, receives "Wedding Song." The Type-C prepares for inspiration with constant, conscious effort.

You have everything you need to become a Type-C creator of collisions. Here's all you need to do:

1. Stuff your head with Ping-Pong balls. Expose yourself to ideas, experiences, images and language. Absorb, interact, reflect. Read rapaciously. Pay attention to what's going on around you. Go to concerts and fix carburetors and wrestle greased pigs. Immerse yourself in the kind of writing you want to create.

2. Turn on the wind machine. Allow and encourage those Ping-Pong balls to bump into each other. Put ideas and images together, just to see what might happen. Play "What if?" and "How come?" and "I wonder. . . ." Ask all manner of questions, stupid or otherwise.

Do some of your wondering and wandering on paper. The process of writing will change and enrich the search.

Don't try to control the process. If you do, you can only get the answers you already know, and those won't be the answers you need.

3. Give yourself a sack to put it all in. Call them whatever you will—"concepts" if you're of a more formal turn of mind, "notions" or "hunches" if you're more of a shirtsleeves thinker, "solutions" if you're a problem solver. Whatever you call them, you'll get them, dozens of them a day, more than any ten creative geniuses could use in ten lifetimes.

And you'll lose them, too, unless you provide yourself with sacks to stick them in. Don't wait for inspiration to strike before striking out on a writing project. Start the project; the sparks and flares and couplings will begin to cluster around that project, and you'll find yourself layering your writing with new inspiration, going back to the beginning and creating it anew, watching the project grow almost as if on its own.

If You Write It, Inspiration Will Come

In *Field of Dreams*, a voice told Ray Kinsella that "if you build it, he will come." So Kinsella mowed down his cornfield and built a baseball diamond—strictly on faith. He didn't even know who the "he" would be. Kinsella built it, and several "he's" came, first legendary baseball player Shoeless Joe Jackson and a few of his All-Star friends, and then Kinsella's long-dead father, bringing a ball, a glove and reconciliation.

Notice the sequence here. First you build; then the miracles show up. You don't wait for the miracle and then start building. Write first. Inspiration will come.

The Law of Entropy Repealed

I started this project with a title and a contract to write a book. I had no outline, so I began to write an outline, and the outline came. I've revised it often, to fit the writing that has emerged, but the outline I started with was enough to get me started.

I labeled file folders, one per chapter, and stashed newspaper and magazine clippings and notes scrawled on envelopes, bookstore receipts and phone bills. The folders gave me places to stick the ideas. Knowing that I had the places, I got the ideas, and I wrote them down before they escaped. I wrote them just as they occurred to me, without trying to shape them or to make them fit the structure that was developing for the book.

Each chapter got a "folder" on a disk in the Macintosh magic box, too. Chapters grew in layers and by bursts. I never considered a chapter finished just because I'd written it and gone on to something else. I've been in and out of chapters constantly over the last several months, adding, trimming, moving.

I didn't write the chapters in the order they now appear. I wrote them as they revealed themselves to me. Had I made them wait their turn, they might have wandered off before their turns ever came.

The whole world has conspired to help me write this book. I've read voraciously, attended seminars, sat in on classes, and much of what I've read and heard and interacted with has been just what I needed for the book—before I even knew that I needed it, before I knew that it existed. Once you build the diamond, the players show up. Once you start the project, the ideas arrive.

According to the Law of Entropy, order tends toward chaos, creation toward disintegration; in general, according to the theory, the universe is winding down toward inevitable dissolution. Son Jeremiah offers this addendum: If left alone, a room will always tend to become messier, never neater.

I think Jeremiah's right about rooms. I can't speak to the nature of the universe. But I can tell you with certainty that the Law of

Entropy doesn't apply to the Type-C writer. I offer, instead, the *Law of Fecundity*: Chaos and random collisions, if given a project to cluster around, will produce ever more and better ideas.

Cultivating Creativity

Humans were first hunters and gatherers, moving with the herds and the seasons. About nine thousand years ago, we figured out that we could tame animals and plants, so we could always have a ready supply of food.

Some folks—a university professor/botanist named Jonathan Sauers and an entrepreneur named Ed Janus among them—argue that we first cultivated grain to brew beer, not to bake bread, making beer the foundation for civilization.

Whatever the motive, once we started cultivating our food instead of having to chase it down, two-car garages and crab grass were but a short step away.

Up to now, we've pretty much hunted our creativity in the wild. But some have learned to plant, cultivate and harvest their creativity, to prepare the soil and nurture the shoots, so that the food of creative inspiration is always available.

You can cultivate your creativity by fostering those internal collisions and embracing your new ideas when they occur. You'll need to work not only on preparing yourself internally to accept inspiration but also on creating an external environment where those wild oats can flourish. If you are the seed from which creativity will grow, you must also have good soil to grow in.

Carl Rogers says we need two things outside of ourselves to allow our creativity to flourish: *psychological safety* and *psychological freedom*.

A sense of psychological safety comes from an environment in which we feel accepted unconditionally as worthy. We need empathy, not evaluation, to thrive.

A kid sometimes gets that kind of unconditional acceptance from parents. Not that we don't instruct and reprimand our kids. But ultimately, we always love them, right or wrong, good or bad, and the kid senses this acceptance.

As adults, we may find this kind of nurturing at home, where we can be accepted for who and what we are. If we're very lucky, we may also find that acceptance at work. Some seek it in a writers' group, where everyone grapples with and understands common problems.

Psychological freedom involves knowing that you can think, feel and express yourself honestly. You have permission to be wrong, to make mistakes, to be afraid and confused, to not know all the answers. Again, you may find this permission at home, at work, in a group, with an individual, perhaps only within yourself.

Permission isn't the same as permissiveness. Permissiveness provides an excuse to fall short of what you're capable of creating or even to quit trying altogether. Permission allows you to transcend the mistakes and the confusion and thus drives you to continue to seek the answers you must have, the new creations you were born to make.

You must find that sense of freedom to make mistakes. If you don't feel it, if you feel only fear of judgment, you won't take chances. If you don't take chances, you won't create.

Keeping in shape to create. Lately I've been doing a lot of writing on medical topics. This should offer you further proof, if you need it, that a freelance writer needn't be an expert to write about a topic. You'll find no medical degrees hiding on my résumé, and in fact, if you looked at my transcript closely, you'd find that I took "physical science" in college to fulfill the lab science requirement in the least scientific manner possible.

But I've had the opportunity to talk to folks who study our heads, our bodies and our hearts. I've interviewed experts on sleep disorders, heart attacks and stress, to folks who test drugs on people and people on drugs, to people who repair the damage life extracts on our bodies and our psyches. I even talked to a researcher who studies the effect of stress on the immune system by separating baby rhesus monkeys from their mothers and then counting their white blood cells.

Near the end of each interview with each expert, I ask the same question: "What should we do in order to live as healthy, happy and productive a life as possible?"

No matter what the discipline, the background or the bias of the expert, they all tell me the same thing. An expert on sleep disorders, Dr. Steven Weber, calls it "boring rules for healthy living." They sound a lot like the advice your mother probably gave you. If so, momma knew best.

Boring Rules for Healthy Living

1. Eat and drink right. Ellen calls it "the tree bark and prunes diet." Basically, it's high fiber/low fat, and every expert I've talked to recommends it. To keep your heart, colon and other body parts happy, eat lots of fruits, vegetables and grains, and stay away from sugars and fats.

Water is highly underrated and underused; we should drink six to eight glasses a day.

Booze is highly overrated and overused, especially as a relaxant or sleep inducer. A lot of doctors I spoke with urged flat-out total abstinence. A few libertines would allow one drink a day.

The jury is still out on caffeine. Nobody recommended it as a health tonic, but several said it has pretty well been cleared of charges that it contributes to cancer or heart disease. You can get hooked on it though, and too much of it at the wrong time can prevent you from getting the second item on your good health list.

2. Get enough rest. Sleep experts disagree on how much is enough. Many, like the University of Wisconsin-Madison's Weber, maintain that just about all of us need eight hours of sleep in any given twenty-four-hour period, although we will vary widely as to when we want that sleep. "Early to bed and early to rise" suits me just fine, but midnight coyotes like Weber find nighttime to be the best time to be active.

Other experts, like the Mayo Clinic's Dr. Peter Hauri, describe a much wider range of "normal" sleeping patterns, with "short sleepers" needing as few as two or three hours of sleep per twenty-four and "long sleepers" needing nine, ten or more.

But the experts agree that most of us aren't getting as much sleep as we need. If you tend to doze off the moment you sit down, fatigue is probably cutting your productivity and making you grouchy.

Experts recommend that we establish a regular sleep pattern and stick to it. If you change your sleep habits radically on the weekend, for example, you'll knock your internal sleep-clock out of whack.

Insomnia is a lot like writer's block. The more you worry about it, the more you create it. Relax. If you can't sleep, get up and do something else for a while. But get up at the scheduled time the next morning. Keep doing that, and after a few nights the problem will generally resolve itself.

3. Take time out. Stress can make you sick. The fellow with the rhesus monkeys and other researchers are finding direct links between stress and various diseases, from arthritis to some forms of cancer. Stress doesn't create the disease, but it does lower our ability to fight the disease off.

For a long time, we assumed that the people in the highest positions of authority — the CEOs of major corporations, for example — endured the highest stress levels on the job. But research now indicates that the folks in the middle — middle managers, high school teachers, secretaries — have the highest stress levels and the highest levels of stress-related illness. It's a matter of control. The less control you feel you have over your life, the more stress you endure.

Life can deliver gut-wrenching stress away from the job, too, in the form of the death of a loved one, the break up of a relationship or other trauma. But even good change — achievement, a long-anticipated move or successfully going on a diet, for example — can be stressful.

To combat stress, rest is almost as important as sleep. Take a break during your workday, or else your body will simply keep winding up tighter and tighter.

You may want to study the works of Dr. Maxie Maultsby or other cognitive therapists, who can teach you how to change your negative thinking and take control of your responses to stressful situations.

If stress gets out of control, it may develop into a full-fledged anxiety disorder. Panic attacks come in many varieties and include a number of physical symptoms, among them rapid heartbeat, the shakes, profuse sweating, and nausea. Some folks get such severe attacks, they are rendered unable to move for durations ranging from several minutes to hours at a time.

If you suffer from such attacks, you may need medication to combat the debilitating symptoms while you learn how to bring your stress levels under control. But for most of us, the simple process of taking time out for a little deep breathing and mental roving will do a wonderful job of bringing the stress levels down.

4. Get your body moving. Instead of simply sitting with your feet up during that rest break, incorporate exercise into your daily schedule. A work-out shows up on everybody's keep-well list. We're not talking about training for the Iron Man Marathon. We're talking about training for life, about keeping head and heart and body functioning well, about keeping the doors open to creative inspiration and then being fit enough to capitalize on those inspirations.

Find something you like and stick with it—swimming, brisk walking, cycling, anything that gets your heart pumping and has you sucking wind. Vary your activities, if necessary, to maintain your interest and also to maximize the benefits. Build exercise into your daily life. Don't let it be a matter of *if*; make it a matter of *when*.

Most folks find that regular exercise, rather than sapping them of energy, actually energizes them. It also cranks up the metabolism for several hours afterward, making it easier to lose weight or maintain your target weight once achieved. And it even promotes restful, refreshing sleep, as long as you don't exercise too soon before bedtime.

It all seems to tie together. Every item on the fitness list helps you to achieve every other item on the list, and all of them together help you function at your best.

Functioning at your best means promoting lots of creative collisions and then letting your wild notions carry you to new creations.

Not Good-Bye,
Never Good-Bye

What really knocks me out is a book that, when
you're all done reading it, you wish the author that
wrote it was a terrific friend of yours and you could
call him up on the phone whenever you felt like it.
—J.D. Salinger, writing as Holden Caulfield, Catcher in the Rye

This summer, while I let this manuscript simmer for three weeks,
Ellen, Rosie and I took a 5,500-mile drive. We visited many of our
country's prominent attractions — Yellowstone, Mt. Rushmore, the
Corn Palace in Mitchell, South Dakota, the Cody Museum in Cody,
Wyoming, Ike's birthplace in Abilene, Kansas.

We walked into the corn beyond center field in the "Field of
Dreams" outside Dyersville, Iowa.

We even went to a Hard Rock Cafe in Las Vegas, so now we
understand what all those T-shirts are about.

We also visited some of the nation's lesser-known wonders — the
one and only library in Oldham County, Texas, the Hot and Cold
water towers in Pratt, Kansas, Sam Lynn Ball Park in Bakersfield,
California, Ricks College in Rexburg, Idaho. One hot, dusty morning, we drove up the Bighorn Mountains outside of Sheridan, Wyoming, encountering near the peak a shepherd and his flock.

We quickly established a routine. My most important duties centered on taking Rosie for an early walk and making coffee. The road
imposed its rhythms on us, and for twenty-one days highway maps
and rest stops pretty much defined the limits of our lives.

I stood on the second floor balcony of a Best Western Motel in
Sundance, Wyoming, watching the dawn hitting the cliffs to the
west, and realized that I was forming a picture in my mind that
would never go away. I would mentally revisit Sundance, and Vega,

Texas, and Van Meter, Iowa, often when I returned to "my" world of Madison, Wisconsin.

I was away from most of the things I use to define myself—my routines, my home, my writing and teaching, my coffeehouse and my union terrace. If I'm not where I usually am, doing what I usually do—and having breakfast in a diner in Kansas where all the other patrons are wearing spurs, I'm most decidedly not myself—then who am I? Can I still write if reduced to notebook and pen instead of magic box and floppy disk?

At home, I sometimes mistake all my patterns for myself. When I got away from those patterns, my shadow selves emerged, stretching and blinking, for an airing. I found myself thinking new thoughts, writing in new ways in my journal.

It's nice to have discipline and routine, to have tools that help me to write more and, I dare to hope, better. But it's nice to shatter the routine occasionally, to throw away the tools and start over.

Writing Upside Down and Backward

Before the Macintosh magic box, even before Ottmar Mergenthaler's magnificent Linotype, a printer set type by hand, a letter at a time, upside down and backwards. Many country editors composed their copy that way, eliminating the middle step.

I learned to handset type as a boy. You hold the stick in one hand and stand before the two cases, upper case for capitals, lower for, well, lower case (and yes, that's why we call them that). Learning the upper case is easy because the little stalls are arranged in alphabetical order. But the lower case presents a challenge. The most frequently used letters—*e, t, a, i, s, n, h* and *r*—are stored in the biggest boxes and are closest at hand. That makes sense, a lot more sense than the keyboard, but you still have to learn the case. Sure, you can mark the boxes—although a real printer would look upon the practice with disdain—but as long as you have to look, you'll never attain any speed.

So you have to just plunge in, learning by doing, being careful not to confuse your p's and your q's (and yes, that's where we got that expression, too)—until finally your hands get smart and learn to fly to the right little boxes without the brain having to send them.

You have to set the words upside down and backward so they'll read right when printed. You fill the stick—about twelve lines of type—and transfer the type to a galley. You make space between the lines by inserting narrow strips of lead, shorter than the type so they won't print. We still call the space between the lines "leading" (pronounced "ledding") after this practice. Then you ink the type with a roller, press a page on it and "pull a galley proof" to check for errors. Finally, you lock all the columns of type into a chase, and you're ready to print.

■■■■■■■■■■■■■■■■■■■■■
Exploration: Writing With Hammer and Chisel

 If you want to look at your writing in a new way, try performing the physical act of writing in a new way. If setting type by hand seems a bit too involved, try something simpler. If you're accustomed to a keyboard, compose in long hand. If you already write longhand, use your off-hand. Clutch a crayon instead of a ball point and scrawl on butcher paper.

You'll be like a kid learning to express thoughts in words on paper for the first time. By getting in touch with that genius kid inside you, you'll be releasing the master writer to do more original, more honest and more interesting writing.

Next I'll Be Subscribing to the *National Enquirer*

As adolescents, we go through a second great stage of self-definition, an "I am not you" phase equal in intensity to the one that makes the terrible twos such a trial for all concerned. Teenagers throw off parental values to assert their own. That we later reembrace many of the values we grew up with doesn't negate the importance of this rebellion. Far from it. We must reject imposed values if we are to truly value anything.

In part, we're really refinding ourselves, rediscovering attitudes, desires and inclinations we had as kids. (I suspect we're born with a lot of them.) The process goes on for a long time, probably all our lives.

We must be careful not to define ourselves too narrowly. In creating a consistent, integrated self to present to the world, we might leave out a lot of the good stuff. We must maintain what my writer friend Kate Loftus calls our writer's "peripheral vision," our awareness of what's at the edges of self, breaking clear of our tunnel vision.

Ellen bought a copy of *Cosmopolitan* this summer. She reads trash mags on vacation, a marvelous practice. The cover blurb started at the sultry model's right ear and tumbled down to just above her elbow: "What nice married women fantasize about — naughty but nice."

What garbage, I sniffed. I don't read junk like that.

But it was around, and I'd read all the local papers, and nobody was looking and . . . oh, all right, I was kind of curious as to what married women *do* fantasize about. (Not, I presumed correctly, their husbands.) So I read *Cosmo*. And once I got over the sense that I was doing something I shouldn't have been, I found it a lot like traveling through a strange town and trying to find the best place to get a good cup of coffee. I didn't know my way around, but the basic terrain was familiar enough.

I'm not likely to become a regular *Cosmo* reader. Something tells me I don't quite fit the reader profile. But the vacation from my regular reading stretched me a bit.

You don't find yourself, after all. You find your *selves*, lots of them. And you do it in part by forgetting self and by shedding the learned, imposed and assimilated false selves.

At the moment of creation, the forgetting becomes profound. Set the self aside totally, becoming absorbed in the writing, and in that moment find your true self.

Until We Meet Again

Your houseguests are finally leaving. You try not to smile too broadly as you see them off.

"This isn't good-bye," you assure each other. "It's only 'until we meet again.' "

They've been quite a chore, really, disrupting your routine, messing up your house, demanding your attention. And yet, the house feels mighty empty and quiet without them. You catch yourself missing them.

I feel that way about finishing this book for you. Writing it has been time-consuming and demanding. It has assuredly kept me away from other things I'd like to be doing. And yet . . . I've enjoyed our prolonged conversation very much, and life will seem empty without it.

I'll probably do what I did after I finished *Freeing Your Creativity* — start another book. So this isn't good-bye but, rather, "until we meet again."

Meanwhile, a few parting words to see you on your journey toward becoming the master writer who is within you.

- Read voraciously. Experience fully. Ask questions always.
- Write from all of yourself — all of your rational, controlling Little Mind and all of your chaotic, creative Big Mind. Write from your happy, spontaneous child and your sure, capable master. Call on all the shadow selves within you.
- Take chances. Think wild thoughts. Trust your kid. Play with words, ideas and images. Create collisions.
- Give yourself permission to make mistakes, to be wrong, to not know. At some point on your journey you'll realize, if you haven't already, that there's really no such thing as a mistake.

You have everything you need inside of you. You can teach yourself everything you need to know. You can write your way into and out of any discovery you need to make. Once you begin, you'll receive more inspiration than you'll ever need.

You will write with the skill of a master and the genius of a child.

Index